perverse
desire
and the
ambiguous
icon

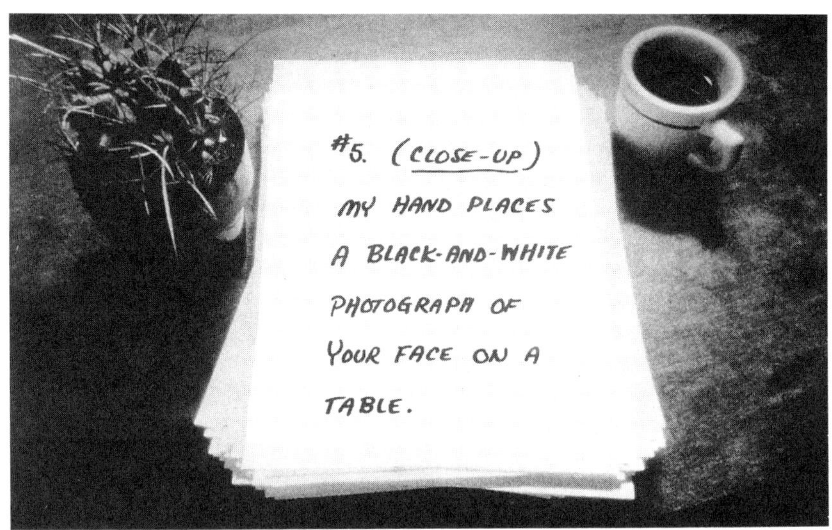

Hollis Frampton, film still from *Poetic Justice* (1972)
Courtesy Anthology Film Archives

perverse desire and the ambiguous icon

allen s. weiss

STATE UNIVERSITY OF NEW YORK PRESS

Production by Ruth Fisher
Marketing by Dana E. Yanulavich

Published by
State University of New York Press, Albany

For information, address the State University of New York Press,
State University Plaza, Albany, NY 12246

Library of Congress Cataloging-in-Publication Data

Weiss, Allen S., 1953–
     Perverse desire and the ambiguous icon / Allen S. Weiss.
         p.   cm.
     ISBN 0-7914-2155-4 (CH).   —ISBN 0-7914-2156-2 (PB)
     1. Aesthetics.   2. Psychoanalysis and art.   I. Title.
   BH301.P78W45   1994
   111'.85—dc20   93-50160
                                                              CIP

10 9 8 7 6 5 4 3 2 1

for Gregory Whitehead
and
Grégoire Testeblanche

I challenge any lover of painting
to love a canvas as much as a
fetishist loves a shoe.

Georges Bataille

contents

acknowledgments

The Introduction was not previously published. (This text appeared in a different and expanded form in my doctoral dissertation, *Subject Construction and Spectatorial Identification: A Revision of Contemporary Film Theory*, Department of Cinema Studies at New York University, 1989, directed by Annette Michelson.)

"Iconology and Perversion" was originally published as a monograph of the same title (Malvern, Australia: Art & Text Publications, 1988); it is reprinted here by the gracious permission of the publisher, Paul Foss.

"Compulsive Beauty" originally appeared in *Alea* 2 (1992).

"Innate Totems" was not previously published.

"Pressures of the Sun" first appeared in *Continuum* 6, no. 1 (1992), an issue on "Radio-Sound" edited by Toby Miller; it also appeared under the title "Artaud in Mexico" in *Lusitania* 1, no. 4 (1993), a special issue on "The Abject, America," edited by Catherine Liu.

"Between the Desire and the Spasm" was published in *Contemporary French Civilization* 16, no. 2 (1992), an issue on "Discourses and Sex" edited by Lawrence Schehr.

"Formations of Subjectivity and Sexual Identity" was published in *Cinema Journal* 28, no. 1 (1988); this essay won first prize in the Society for Cinema Studies Student Essay Contest; it is reprinted by permission of the Board of Trustees of the University of Illinois. (This chapter appeared in slightly different form in my doctoral dissertation.)

"Acting, Identity, and Scenarization" was published in *Art & Text* 34 (1989), a special issue on "New Paradigms in Film

Theory" edited by Allen S. Weiss. (This text also appeared in different form in my doctoral dissertation.)

"Lucid Intervals" was published in *Continental Philosophy III* (Routledge, 1990), an issue on "Postmodernism—Philosophy and the Arts" edited by Hugh Silverman; it is reprinted by courtesy of the publisher, Routledge, Chapman and Hall, Inc.

"Broken Voices, Lost Bodies" was not previously published.

The revised translations from Antonin Artaud's *Artaud le Mômo* are from Clayton Eshleman, *Conductors of the Pit* (New York: Paragon House, 1988). They are reprinted with the kind permission of the author.

All texts are corrected and revised.

introduction: on a certain melancholy of theory

Certain spirits who love mystery want to believe that objects conserve something of the eyes that behold them . . .
—Marcel Proust, *Le temps retrouvé*

A flyer advertising the prominent film journal *Wide Angle* featured a "teaser" consisting of a photograph of Marlene Dietrich with a caption that reads: "DIETRICH: Her 'difference' concealed by fetishization, the woman presents no threat to the male subject," a quotation from Kaja Silverman's article, "Lost Objects and Mistaken Subjects: Film Theory's Structuring Lack."[1] This advertisement is a sort of inadvertant pastiche of a central theme from one of the seminal articles of current psychoanalytically oriented film theory, Laura Mulvey's "Visual Pleasure and Narrative Cinema," which appeared nearly a decade earlier in *Screen*.[2] In order to indicate certain problematic aspects of the theoretical issues at stake, it is worth taking a closer look at this photograph and rereading the caption with some attention to both visual detail and received opinion.

The photograph shows Dietrich in the classical Dietrich style: high-heeled shoes laced up on her calves, black stockings, skirt hitched all the way up to her crotch, low-cut black bodice, and her most alluring bodily posture and facial expression. Isn't this the modern, cinematic archetype of the femme fatale, of the castrating (and not castrated) woman? Isn't this (on the iconic, even before the narrative, level) precisely the type of woman who poses the greatest threat to the male (not to mention the female) subject? And what of her "difference"? Why is this term placed in single quotes? Isn't the female subject somehow different from the male subject (and the female image from the male image)? Who, after having bothered to look at this photograph, can really say that this difference (without quotation marks) is truly concealed!? This photograph would rather seem to be an epitome of the pictorial representation of sexual difference. As for the claim that her "difference" is concealed by fetishization, more on this topic later; let it suffice for the moment to note that within the bounds of classic psychoanalytic theory: (1) fetishization does not completely conceal sexual difference; (2) fetishization is a particular (and not generalized) psychopathological symptom; (3) it makes little sense to speak of the entire female body (as object of desire) as a fetish object; (4) fetishism is a mode of psychic activity and not a general set of characteristics pertaining to a given category of objects. All of this might lead us to suspect that if Dietrich were really "tamed" in this film, it would be a function of narrative resolution and not of a specific type of iconic representation. At least not this particular icon, and certainly not in the manner indicated by the caption.

Who could have made such an implausible, indeed outrageous, claim? Perhaps a copyeditor or publicist not quite familiar with the theoretical works in question. Certainly a theoretician! The same page of this flyer informs us that *Wide Angle* is a journal that "presents diverse critical analyses, including formalist, feminist, and psychoanalytical approaches to film theory." We know, through the vast literature on the topic, what is crucial here for film theory, especially feminist film theory. Indeed, the coming of age of film theory, cinema studies, art history, and cultural studies necessitated a viable synthesis of the diverse modes of film theory and their feminist instances.

The necessity of a vigorous polemic intended to ensure the entry of that discourse into the mainstream is obvious and imperative. But polemic must not be confused with theory, and it must be remembered that the rationalization and universalization of theoretical discourse is always an assumption of power, in a reflexive mode of self-justification. Though there is a certain power specific to the cinematic object—stemming from visual pleasure and fascination—there is also a quite different power specific to theorization. The latter power derives from logical and rhetorical authority, structured by the "arts" of persuasion. A sign of this theoretical power play is the rise of metatheory, the theorization about theorization, which always reveals a certain anxiety about truth. It is at precisely this level that the original object, the artwork, is often lost. Hence the possibility of writing such a caption: the object (in this case, the photograph of Dietrich) no longer serves as image, as representation, as icon, but rather as the sign or emblem of a theoretical position, as an incitement to theorize. Cinema studies is beset not by what Paul de Man called the "resistance to theory,"[3] but rather by a compulsion to theorize (from which the present text is no exception). But all too often, in losing its object, this compulsion to theorize produces textual monsters or grotesqueries, created by the extreme inbreeding of self-reflection. These must not be summarily discarded, since they are the sign or symptom of the state of our criticism; they must rather be treated with the irony, or perhaps with the Duchampian "meta-irony," that they deserve. It is not the sleep of reason, but rather an excess of reason, that produces these monsters.

In terms of classical mainstream cinema, this problematic leads to the vicious hermeneutic circle of spectatorship, pleasure, profit, production, spectatorship. . . . To make the destruction of cinematic pleasure a tactical, rhetorical, polemical moment of the struggle (a hyperbolic use of theory and discourse necessary for all revolutionary or revisionist activity) is justified by the radical need to change the world. Yet to transform this very same valorization of displeasure into a universalized theoretical principle is precisely to fall into the traps of psychic bureaucratization. Why this ascesis? Cannot the ends of pleasure be directed? Why need they be necessarily malevolent? Can we not posit a mode of enjoying beautiful bodies, female and male, which would not be detrimental to the feminist struggle? Can there not be a new way of seeing, a new logic of the gaze, which breaks the bonds of sexism, racism, nationalism; a model according to which such pleasures would receive new meaning and a definite political approbation?

If vision were intrinsically phallocentric, as Lacanian theory would have us believe, then all polemicization or theorization whatsoever about the cinema would be futile. The only way out of this ideological impasse would then be to valorize the nonvisual arts (as was the case, for example, in the iconophobic and iconoclastic limits of the Judeo-Christian traditions) or to institutionalize blindness. We might anecdotally recall here that Kafka found it particularly appropriate that one of the cinema theaters in Prague, named for the charitable association that sponsored it, was called the Cinema of the Blind. Believing that cinema "concentrates one's eyes on the superficial," Kafka remarked: "Cinema of the Blind! Every cinema should be called that. Their flickering images blind people to reality!"[4] Film theory, if not bankrupt, would be at least futile.

In question here are the limits of the application of psychoanalytic theory to aesthetics, and precisely the utilization of the model of fetishization for the understanding of the ideological effects of the cinematic apparatus. Neither these effects nor the debased role of women in Western systems of representation caused by the stylization of the male gaze are in question: merely a certain use of psychoanalytic theory as an interpretive system. Also, the present critique does not intend to question either the empirical validity or the symptomatological accuracy or the metapsychological consistency of the theory of fetishism, but merely a certain mode of its application beyond the strictly psychotherapeutic domain. Thus the present series of essays is intended to serve as a critique of a common category error in film theory, and indeed in all types of aesthetic discourse.

Even granted the accuracy of Mulvey's description of fetishism and of the representation of women in the classic Hollywood film, and the effects of the male gaze and the suturing effect of certain filmic constructions, and the ideological effects of all of the above, what would it mean to speak of the cinematic image as bearing the "fetishistic representation of the female image"? Fetishism, in Freudian metapsychology, is understood as a particular psychological syndrome, as one possible resolution of a psychic trauma. It is not a generalized mode of psychic activity, and certainly not a necessary stage of the ontogenetic psychic process. Fetishism is not a general psychological condition, but a perverse (i.e., structurally and statistically abnormal or marginal) outcome of a certain blockage of personal development. It is, in short, at worst a personality disorder and at best a marginalized erotic syndrome.

Certainly not all representations of fragmented bodies are fetish objects. Simply stated, a shoe may serve as a fetish, but not all shoes are fetish objects. Fetishism is a psychic state and not the definition of a category of objects. If the banality will be excused: fetishism is in the eyes of the beholder. It is the fetishist who constitutes an object as a fetish and not the fetish object that somehow motivates a fetishistically oriented gaze. It is not the cinematic spectacle that creates the fetishistic response to castration anxiety; this response was inaugurated by a much earlier, much more site/sight specific scene or trauma, according to Freud's demonstration.[5] The cinema may represent the fetish, but it can in no way create it. It may perhaps reinforce its effects, but only for the spectator who is already of a fetishistic disposition.

The implied or putative spectator is an ideal spectator; but the very existence of interpretation means that this ideal is often not congruent with the empirical spectator's motivation for being fascinated by the spectacle. The ideal seldom coincides with the empirical. We can postulate a fetishistically organized spectacle which might (but most probably won't) incite the fetishist to greater passions. But we are not all fetishists, and no degree of aesthetic (or theoretical) fascination will change that fact. Thus the psychoanalytically oriented theoretical scenario may be true, but only for an extremely limited number of spectators. We may cite Bataille on this point: "I challenge any lover of painting to love a canvas as much as a fetishist loves a shoe."[6] The fetishist would probably prefer to remain at home polishing his shoes than go to the cinema and see Dietrich's black-laced high-heeled wonders. To argue for the hypothetical existence of an ideal subject position implied by the spectacle does not necessarily entail the empirical spectator's fascination by that spectacle, by that ideal: many are left cold.

Don't give the cinema a power that it doesn't have; don't give film theory a power that *it* doesn't have. The mode of fascination particular to the fetish object is not the same as that particular to the cinema, even if the cinema can in fact represent that very same fetishism, and even if the cinematic apparatus bears certain fundamental structural similarities with fetishization (and voyeurism). This aspect of psychoanalytic film analysis falls into an archaic epistemological model: resemblance. We must analyze the similarities and differences between the cinematic apparatus and the psychic apparatus, all the while avoiding the epistemological trap of deducing causal relations from structural homologies.[7]

The differences between the formation of films and fetishes may reveal some key features of the problematic of sublimation. The filmic image is a construct and not a projection of a psychic state or a "mirror." What is "projected" by the spectator onto the scenario of the film may at times coincide with the ideal spectator posited by the film's narrative and iconic structures, but this is not necessarily so. The complicated problem of identification in film theory must be addressed: there is no spectator *simpliciter,* male or female. In terms of the present analysis, this means that to speak of "a spectator" or "an audience" would imply totally different hermeneutic paradigms. Furthermore, identification is always partial, fragmented, mixed; total identification would be delirium.

Hence the possibility, and the definite interest, of misinterpretation. The filmic text is certainly, though only partially, symptomatic of the psychological state of the *auteur,* (whatever combination of creativity and stereotyping, and whatever conglomorate of persons and institutions, this term may designate.) Yet such symptoms are secondary to the meaning of the filmic text, a meaning which the film projects into the future of every spectator. The film is both autofigurative and figurative; both object and representation; both artwork and symptom. To understand the author we can treat the film as symptom; to understand the film we must treat it as text. Its symptomatic qualities may be germane to this task, but are not necessarily so. Every film is in some sense a documentary about something (due to photography's representational, iconic facility), but no film is a priori documentary, due to its nature as artifice. We must not confuse film criticism with psychotherapy, nor ascribe the powers of the analyst to those of the filmmaker or the film. One cannot psychoanalyze an artwork, only a person.

As Roland Barthes eloquently explains: "The novel is in effect a faked *mathesis,* leading to a misappropriation [*détournement*] of knowledge."[8] This is equally true for film, as well as for theory, despite the common desire to conceal the narrative effects of theorization. Criticism, theory, and the cinema itself can indeed serve the purposes of a revolutionary praxis, to "unfix" the spectator and to liberate the gaze. This has always been, of course, the aim of a certain radical psychotherapeutic procedure. But, as Christian Metz has demonstrated, the film is not a phantasm, though it may have originated in phantasms and may be the source of innumerable others. Criticism, theory, and the cinema may serve as a sort of resolution, as *revelateur,* of these psychic processes. But the possibilities of psychic/filmic inmixing are as numerous as the combinatory formed by multiplying all possible cinematic forms by all possible psychic syndromes—if not infinite, these possibilities are at least of indefinite number.

In a particularly Brechtian tone, Mulvey poses the task of a radical, alternative cinema as being the disruption of certain aesthetic conventions whereby the task would be to free, "the look of the audience into dialectics, passionate detachment," adding that, "there is no doubt that this destroys the satisfaction, pleasure and privilege of the 'invisible guest.' . . ."[9] We, the spectators, are the invisible guests; I, for one, cannot imagine going to the movies if there is to be no pleasure attached to that activity. Theory will save me from ideology: the most insidiously reactionary film (which might also be the most intensely pleasurable one!) poses little threat once deconstructed. Once analyzed for its ideological content and threat, we can then enjoy it for one aspect of what it is, an aesthetic object, while understanding it in terms of another aspect of what it is, a sociological artifact. The appreciation of one aspect does not imply the neglect of the other. The guest might be invisible, but this does not mean naive: the call for "passionate detachment" is perhaps not so different from that "willing suspension of disbelief" posited by Coleridge as a key feature of the aesthetic experience. The difference is in the radical contemporary desire for an aesthetic asceticism, a strange need to exorcize pleasure from the cinematic experience.

Isn't theory that domain where the passions have already been decathected from their objects? Isn't theory already a caution, an asceticism, a subversive activity? And doesn't it, for just these very reasons, all too often forget its object and insert its own phantasms in the place of that lost object?—as did the author of that caption to the Dietrich photograph discussed at the beginning of this exposé. Theory is, perhaps, "willfulness" applied to a fascinating object; theory is that willfulness which permits "passionate detachment." If the filmic object were simply a symptom, then we would not need psychoanalytic theory, but psychotherapeutic sessions, to decathect. This doesn't seem to be the case: otherwise all theory itself would be but a futile, spurious attempt at liberation; otherwise rationality would be undifferentiated from pure phantasms, and would have no causal efficacy. But it does—often to our great distress.

In conclusion, let us return to Proust:

> Certain spirits who love mystery want to believe that objects conserve something of the eyes that behold them, that monuments and paintings appear to us only under the sensible veil woven by the love and contemplation of so many admirers over the centuries. This chimera would become true if they transposed it into the domain of each person's unique reality, into the domain of each person's own sensibility. Yes, in this sense, and only in this sense (but it is much greater), a thing that we have previously looked at, if seen again, brings back to us, along with the gaze we had set upon it, all the images it previously contained. It's that the things—a book under its red cover like all the others—as soon as they are perceived by us, become something immaterial within us, of the same nature

> as all our preoccupations and all our feelings of that ear-
> lier time, and are indissolubly mingled with them.[10]

Yet the inverse is equally true: there are some people who believe that our souls are imprinted with certain aspects of the
objects captured by the gaze. The difference between these two
claims would amount to the difference between two radically
different theoretical positions: the first where active spectatorial
projection determines the meaning of the artwork (where, as
Duchamp would have it, the spectator is instrumental in com-
pleting the artwork); and the second, authorial and authorita-
tive, would imply that the artwork is an effective propaganda
machine, imprinting its ideology on the passive spectator.

Doesn't the truth of the matter lie at the (impossible? contradictory? dialectical?) intersection of these two extremes, each
of which alone merely serves as a limit case for a unified theoretical stance? Must theory deny the pleasures associated with
these two positions? Taken by itself, Proust's statement would
be antitheoretical; its inverse would be equally so. But the impulse to theorize always permits the possibility (and often entails the necessity) of positing the inverse, counterfactual position as a test case or a corrective. Ultimately, the possibility
of theory is the very possibility of changing the object itself:
theory is a radical task, but as soon as it forgets its object in
the realms of metatheory, as soon as it becomes blind to the
world that it describes, it is no less dangerous than the ideology it purports to criticize. The willfulness of valid theory need
not disengage us from the pleasure of its objects—nor, indeed,
from the very different pleasures of theorization itself. But it
must reveal to us how these pleasures and these theories can
be abused, misplaced, misappropriated. Theory must contain
a nostalgia, must create a wound, to remind us of the loss of
the art object inherent in such theorization.

In his tale, "Tlön, Uqbar, Orbis Tertius," Jorge Luis Borges
explains that, "The metaphysicians of Tlön do not seek for the
truth or even for verisimilitude, but rather for the astounding.
They judge that metaphysics is a branch of fantastic literature."[11] When Freudian metapsychology loses its clinical roots

in certain extremes of theoretical flight and fabulation, it consequently loses its axiomatics, and it too then becomes a sort of fantasy—commendable and politically correct, perhaps, but of dubious hermeneutic efficacy. The fact that metaphysics can inform fantasy is admirable and fascinating, but not for applied theory. I myself would hope to become such a Tlönian metaphysician—but that is the task for another, very different, volume.[12]

1   iconology and perversion: post-psychoanalytic aesthetics

A manifesto, if universally accepted, is nothing but cruel necessity; if unread, it is merely a phantasm. Yet phantasms do not exist within intercalary moments, but in history, where the "cunning of reason" (Hegel) engenders coherence from chance, contingency, chaos. Whence the paradox of all expression, political or otherwise: discourse is inadequate to its causes (desires) and is exceeded by its effects (texts, events). Art obeys the laws of productive desire in a realm of pure volition, irrespective of the axiomatics of rationalized reality, while aesthetic theory and criticism provide the articulation of the structural "laws" of art and the "logic" of historical events. Our icons and symbols are residues of the gaze and the world's visibility, based on phantasms and restricted by history. When these icons are transformed into idols or truths, difference is abolished and the violence of universal reason is unleashed. That uniformity, that statistical leveling of value, is the historical form of modern, technocratized rationality.

Culture, once it becomes aligned with capital, follows the statistical curves of the various economic and political laws of averages, where the new paradigms of cultural realities are those of marketing and pari-mutuel betting. Freedom itself is the greatest threat to freedom: the double bind of democracy is that in a media-oriented epoch, cultural value becomes a function of the representation of *stereotypical* symbolic phantasmagoria. At this time, perversion—through its ability to side with the unique passions against universal reason and totalization—can offer a subversive possibility, a contentious measure, a countertradition whereby difference is guaranteed and maintained. Difference is at the foundation of all possible hermeneutics, of all interpretation; for what is interpretation if not the projection of difference?

Ultimately, such a strategy should contest the presumption of speaking for the other in the name of reason or of common sense, a presumption which in effect would be to silence the other. This silence is precisely the subtle, veiled violence of reason. We must seek different paradigms, different test cases, different ideals which permit the liberation of alterity. Perversion must be subversive, or it will no longer be.

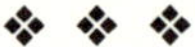

Nietzsche teaches that, as a condition of being "human, all too human," the world is a host of errors and phantasms. We might take one particularly willful error as our theme and speculate upon the phantasms which sustain it. In a certain French convent, today, the novices permit themselves a perverse literary amusement. During the evening meal, as the others eat, one novice is entrusted with reading, out loud and in Latin, the *Lives of the Saints*. The game is to add additional tortures to the multitude already suffered by the martyrs, in such a manner as to escape notice of the spiritual director supervising the reading. Willful error or perverse phantasm? Within the theological context of the convent and the exigencies of the novitiate, the bodies of Christ and the martyrs serve not merely religious ends. They also populate the imaginative scenarios which proffer the corporeal surfaces on which are inscribed the most varied and extreme sadomasochistic phantasms, and from which radiate the most sublime beatitude. Before permitting any heuristic or hermeneutic operation whatsoever, these inscriptions are the mark of aesthetic pleasure.

It would be a mistake to understand the novices' little game as simply a hypocritical amusement, where the textual pleasure of their "literary" hagiographical inventions would be dissociated from the historical and theological reality of the martyrs' suffering. Rather, the forms of torture delineate forms of pleasure, however incongruous and illicit their entry into the text may be. We cannot dissociate the textual *description* of torture from its physical *inscription* on the body, as we would, in the abstract, sever a signified from a signifier. The novices' little inventions are precisely a rite of passage, a subtle but transgressive means of entry into a theological system through acknowledging—in a fabulation guided by the rhetorical form of the epitrope[1]—the signs of that system by adding their own variations. To add, subtract, or change a sign in a theological system is to create a heresy; but it is only in relation to the multiplication of heresies that orthodoxy can be established. The heterodoxy of blasphemy, heresy, phantasms, and simple (or complex) errors is the provocation at the origins of orthodoxy.

In 787, the second Nicene Council stipulated that the Incarnation justified, indeed necessitated, the veneration of icons of Christ, the Virgin, the angles and the saints. The iconoclastic denial of such veneration became tantamount to the denial of the Incarnation—the foundation of New Testament theology—and was explicitly heretical. Though iconoclastic outbreaks were to continue for another half-century, 843 marked the triumph of orthodoxy, which was the definitive victory of Christian iconophilia. At stake here was the representation of the human body; the aesthetic vectors of this victory extend through the entire subsequent history of European art, and certainly continue to be experienced today, despite the effects of secularization.

The theoretical debates of the iconoclastic controversy—centered around the differentiation between image and idol—entailed the detailed investigation of several issues which remain central to our epistemological, metaphysical, and aesthetic discourse. Foremost among these issues are: (1) modes of the representation of an original, archetypal object (recollection, typification, analogy, imitation, imaging, etc.); (2) degree of reality of images (simulacrum, idol, phantasm, figure, sign, etc.); (3) types of resemblance (in medieval theology: *imago, similitudo, figura, effigies, facies, pictura*, etc.). A concerted examination of Western church iconography, according to the intricacies of this problematic, would certainly reveal a deeper metaphysical and semiotic level to Western art. The conflict between the Reformation and the Counter-Reformation is but one moment of this history.

An ancient iconoclastic tradition—that of the fourth-century Bishop Epipanius of Salamis—insists that, "it is only in man himself that the divine realities should be engraved, imprinted; it is only in the heart that God should be recalled."[2] Ironically, if taken literally, this dictum evokes not so much the iconoclasm for which it was originally taken, but rather a new relation between icon and incarnation, an iconology of torture, with the Passion as its paradigm and the martyrdom of the saints as its variations. Extrapolated to its logical limit, and serving as a de facto apology for martyrdom, this iconoclasm would excoriate not only images of the divinity, but also that primal source of all imagery, the human body itself. For the inscription of the divine truth upon the body can only destroy that delicate, sensuous surface of our very existence. The exemplary—and symbolic—tortures suffered by the early Christian martyrs would later be appropriated and refined by the church, utilized against *its* enemies in the name of orthodoxy. But before thinking of this as a symbolic system, it must be recognized in its most immediate, harrowing, tormenting reality.

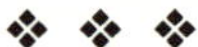

There is a long tradition of symbolization based on the corporeal paradigm, originating in Platonic philosophy, extended through the medieval notion of man-as-microcosm, and delivered unto its contemporary avatars. Freudian metapsychology affirms that, "The ego is first and foremost a bodily ego; it is not merely a surface entity, but is itself the projection of a surface."[3] Thus, as Freud demonstrates earlier in *The Interpretation of Dreams* (1900), all dream imagery symbolizes the body, and all symbolism is ultimately body symbolism. Phenomenological epistemology ascertains the same relations between body and symbol. Merleau-Ponty shows how the body gestalt subtends every other gestalt, how the body "is that strange object which uses its own parts as a general system of symbols for the world."[4] But all such theories function at the level of description, and remain a fortiori representational schemata. The entire problematic of corporeal inscription is neglected, or repressed, except insofar as it is recuperated by the symbolic.

It is rather a certain contemporary tradition of thought—originating in Nietzsche's famous analyses in the second book of *On the Genealogy of Morals* (1887)—which offers an epistemology based upon the analysis of corporeal inscription. Foucault: "The body is the inscribed surface of events (traced by language and dissolved by ideas), the locus of a dissociated Self (adopting the illusion of a substantial unity), and a volume in perpetual disintegration."[5] Lyotard: "The surface, the libidinal skin, is thus already a memory of intensities, a capitalization, a localization of their passages."[6] Here, the idealized gestalt of a "good form" of corporeal unity and symbolic consistency is perpetually disarticulated, decomposed, transgressed.

Libidinal *intensity*, and not a symbolizing *intentionality*, is at the origin of consciousness where, as Nietzsche teaches, memory and gregariousness (and ultimately the symbolic) are instilled by corporeal punishment. Memory is created by blood, torture, and sacrifice: the most originary mnemotechnics insists that, "If something is to stay in the memory it must be burned in."[7] Blood and cruelty are at the very base of rationality itself. All value is, as Deleuze and Guattari explain, a function of the "extraordinary composite of the speaking voice, the marked body, and the enjoying eye,"[8] in a festival of cruelty of the most ancient origins. The body *is* memory, where the wounds inflicted in initiatory ceremonies and vindictive punishments become the scars that remain the trace of one's own suffering, a suffering that creates both self-consciousness and its ethical double, social consciousness.

The anthropologist Pierre Clastres shows how the individual body is marked by the tribal ethos:[9] (1) In the "primitive" legal systems of societies without a state, torture affirms and initiatory scars denote the *interdiction of inequality*; nobody is "worth" more than another. (2) Conversely, in societies with a hierarchized state, punishment ratifies the *interdiction of equality*; the economic, political, and libidinal systems of exchange are based upon unequal values and a disproportionate distribution of powers. Yet in both cases, the use of torture, the forceful marking of the body, transforms the memory of pain into the meaningful sign of the relation of our bodies to the socius. In a culture where the law would be civilized, rational, its signs must be meaningful. The disquieting nature of Kafka's *In the Penal Colony* [1919] is due to the fact that the enunciation of the law as verdict is simultaneous with the act of punishment: the law is inscribed directly on the prisoner's flesh. Furthermore, since the script is so full of embellishments, it is initially illegible; the revelation of the law, by means of deciphering the script through sheer pain, is too little, too late. The advent of meaning is but the prefiguration of death. Here, in the penal colony, far from civilization and with the collapse of tradition, the law as punishment is no longer a social spectacle, and the legal gesture of draconic inscription is transformed into the self-destructive mania of the last keeper of the tradition. There is no text inscribed on his body. The broken machine merely jabs the officer to death: inscription transgresses the boundary of sense, and nonsense is revealed as the mark of death. We may only wonder whether for Kafka this breakdown of meaning is a function of the ultimate sophistry of rational thought, or whether this parable is in fact a footnote to Nietzsche's *On the Genealogy of Morals*, ironically indicating its applicability to nihilistic Western modernity.

The scar turns the body into an icon. The intensity of the knife's passage and the memory of the blood's flow are transformed into a symbol—the mark of passage into society and its regulated systems of value and exchange. These marks transform lived time into historical destiny, where the past (as memory and the unconscious) ordains the future. This passage into culture is the inscription of the phantasmatic upon the symbolic: it is sublimation. Ritualistic tortures are but the signs of this "civilizing" process, indicating the "use value" of the symbolic as a psychic force which instills meaning within us.

But once there is no longer a universal application of initiatory torture, once it enters into the complex machinery of the hierarchized state as an enforcement of the value system, punishment becomes spectacle, theater. The catalogue of torture techniques and devices reveals a specific torture for each part of the body. Torture itself is the most efficient means of disarticulating the body, destroying its form, and turning sensation into a monolithic manifestation of pain, a sign of power. Hanging, whipping, flaying, dismemberment, disembowlment, beheading, garroting, crushing, blinding, breaking, sawing, beating, burning, impaling, drowning, ripping. Axes, saws, whips, scourges, pincers; head-crushers, knee-splitters, breast-rippers, and skull-smashers; thumbscrews, spiked collars, branding irons, mortification belts, breaking wheels; the iron maiden, the heretic's fork, the pendulum and the rack.[10] This is the stuff that creates martyrs (and saintly relics).[11] The sight of such punishments—perhaps symbolically fitting the "crimes"—provides a perverse pleasure. Concluding with the victim's death, such spectacle now serves the spectator as the reminder of a particular fate to be avoided and is no longer the mark of a mnemotechnic procedure which creates a collective destiny. The forgetting of one's own fate is accomplished by the obliteration of another's life; destiny is renounced for spectacle.

We may see here the origins of a perverse aestheticization, perhaps of all aestheticization, as the distanciation of pain through spectacle. The ancient, savage, primitive, barbaric subject is a function of the common inscription of pain directly on the body. But once the application of pain is restricted to one figure in a theological drama (as well as to this figure's saintly avatars), such inscription becomes spectacle, narrative, icon. Modern subjectivity is a function of the reversal of this pain into the pleasures of observation, contemplation, and identification, where the sadomasochistic component of scoptophilia achieves the sublimation of those ancient rites. Sublimation—utilizing all of the rhetorical tricks of the dreamwork, and more—transforms the other's pain into our pleasure, through an affective reversal motivated by the exigencies of guilt and *ressentiment.*

The extreme, indeed fetishistic possibilities of veneration are illustrated by the curious case of a late outbreak of iconoclasm, that of Bishop Claude of Turin, around the year 825. In a quite Borgesian tale, Claude—arguing against the veneration of icons in an attempt to preserve the unity and transcendence of God—claimed that the cross, a horrifying torture instrument, is certainly not a sign of divinity; and if, merely because Christ was nailed to the cross for three hours, we are to venerate the cross, then why not venerate everything that he touched: all virgins, cradles, old linen, boats, donkeys, thorns, lances, etc. And since Christ touched the earth. . . . In a logic moving from metonymic to metaphoric relations, Claude developed, *a contrario* in an *argumentum ad adsurdum,* the limitless possibilities of the veneration of icons and relics in order to ridicule their theological basis. In doing so, he developed a pictorial "logic" not to be fully explored until the Surrealists.

The move from religion or theology to aesthetics is centered on the role of the icon and the experience of the *veneration* of images (as opposed to the *adoration* of God). In conformity with the biblical interdiction against worshiping graven images, the ontological status of icons and their "appreciation" had to be distinguished from that of true worship of the divinity. The paradigmatic formula of this relationship was established by the dictum of the fourth-century Saint Basil the Great: "The honour rendered unto the icon returns to its prototype."[12] Thus authentic worship is a slippage between veneration and adoration, between icon and divinity, between signifier and signified. And it is precisely within the very limits of this slippage that the ambiguities, and heresies, which marked the iconoclastic controversy arose.

Claude of Turin was one of the first theorists of the materiality of the signifier, fully within the Neoplatonic tradition. Considering the representation of man (and divinity) as simulacrum, he concluded that the soul's reduction to the sheer minerality of an image entailed the elimination of man's highest quality: rationality. The image is "dead": the icon is idol. This formula depends upon the confusion between the material and formal aspects of the icon: such is, of course, the question of all visual mediation of the conceptual realm, with the added complication of the relations between the sacred and the secular.

The sensible, corporeal aspect of the icon is hypostatized in its thaumaturgic, miraculous powers. Piety before the icon invokes beneficial miracles; impiety causes calamitous effects. The following anecdote in this regard, recounted at the second Nicene Council, would have inspired Bataille: a certain Harrasin of Gabala struck an icon in the eye, and at that very moment his own eye was enucleated. The apotropaic power of the fetish is equaled by its Medusal potentiality.

The history of the conflict between iconophilia and iconophobia is based on the ontological problematic of the manifestation or representation of the invisible within the visible, the desire to place transcendence in human form (usually in the mode of suffering). Iconolatry or idolatry? Sublimation or perversion? The textual game of our novices—whether blasphemous, heretical, or merely perverse in its hagiographical and psychological implications—is an attempt to change the very order of the theological cosmos, however slightly. One more scar on the martyred body of a saint: a singular passion is manifested in the paranoid order of the sacred universe. These novices wish to participate in creating the scenario and are not content with merely reciting its description. They wish to be authors, artists, creators, and not merely readers, scribes, storytellers. They seek new inscriptions, new intensities, with which to seal their vows.

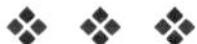

We might better understand these novices' little diversion— and offer it as an allegory for a possible aesthetic model—by reconsidering it in the light of that astounding text dealing with erotic fetishism and love's singularities, Roland Barthes's *A Lover's Discourse* (1977).[13] Erotic love demands that each person discover that unique fetish, that singular object of fascination, which suits one's individual desires. The very possibilities of communication and interpretation are authenticated by the fascination, intoxication, and affirmation that such a love-object evokes, yet all the while the very meaning of this fetish object remains intransigently incommunicable, personal, and ultimately perverse. Psychoanalytic transference: amorous transference = universalized hermeneutics: particularized hermeneutics = *mathesis universalis: poesis singularis.* This analogous thread indicates the significative difference between rational cognition and perverse affect, between sublimated constructions and desublimated phantasms. In contrast to philosophical aesthetics, which constitutes a universalizing hermeneutic procedure, we may posit an anti-universalist practice (mute *pragma* versus loquacious *theoria*) where aesthetic effect is recognized as a function of an ultimately incommunicable phantasm, affect made manifest as a particularized representation. Such affect would operate in regard to the universalized constructs of aesthetic theory as their very internal rupture, as the mark of their very impossibility in the face of the artwork's material particularities and the spectator's psychic singularity.

Fascination—aesthetic or otherwise—is simultaneously a loss of will before the object and an investment of libido in that very same object. The aesthete, like the iconolater and the pervert, seeks the impossible manifestation of the invisible in the visible. It is perhaps this very contradiction as the heart of the visible, supporting iconoclasts and iconophiles alike, which explains a hatred of the aesthetic such as Bataille's, as well as his notion of a "passion of the pure imperative" toward the impossible.[14] This quest—where even the anti-aesthetic attitude is but a reaction to the aesthetic, a countercathexis without preconceived object—entails the notion of the object as catastrophe, as a transitional effect of libidinal cathexes. The form of such "catastrophe" within an ontology of the passions is offered by the notion of a libidinal oscillation between banality and transcendence in the object.[15] All objects are, a priori, overdetermined due to the diverse possibilities of libidinal and hermeneutic investment. The origins of the perverse and the transcendent are one and the same, in that catastrophic, anxiety-producing narcissistic wound from which subjectivity itself arises. In a quest for origins, the bearer of this psychic wound discovers its unique sign in another wound, a corporeal "mutilation" which is to mark the psychic mechanism and the libidinal economy with its own horror, strangeness, excitation. The female sexual orifice (or "slash," if we are to pursue the horrific trail of the libido),

becomes the logical point of departure and symbolic representation of the inaccessible, the unexpressible, the un-
imaginable, the ungraspable, the unreal, the invisible—in
short, of the *unknown relation.* Confronted with this relation, individual reactions may variously be that of horror,
delirium, 'construction,' erotic exaltation, voyeuristic interest, disavowal, phobic flight, denial, disquieting
strangeness, transposition towards epistemophilia by renunciation, etc.[16]

Any object can, in principle, serve as a sign of the possibility of some love or some identification; any object can be
the sign of transcendence, a transcendence which finally traces
the symptomatic disquietude of our very immanence. The limits of the self are defined by the scope and variety of libidinal
cathexes; the range of these cathexes, these passions, is ultimately defined by the manner in which the anguish of the narcissistic wound, and the fear of the sexual wound, are lived
through.

In fetishism, the paradigmatic perversion in psychoanalytic theory, the desired "cult" object circumvents the symbolic
order by threatening the establishment of an alternative law:
the pervert substitutes the law of his desire for the symbolic
law. The very intensity of pleasure—and not the structural coherence of the object's position within the symbolic—is the
lived, corporeal sign and proof that *desire is law.* The pervert's
gaze, marked by the scoptophilic/epistemophilic passion, follows the objects and effects of desire as the signs of a new law.
But if this is the case, wouldn't each perversion be founded
upon a unique passion and offer a singular "iconology"?
Wouldn't a typology of fetishes and perversions be as spurious as those pamphlets which provide the key to the meaning of dream symbols? Wouldn't the psychoanalytic attempt
to ground the theory of perversion on castration anxiety—and
the theory of fetishism on the phantasmatic construct of a female phallus as ego defense mechanism—be merely another
attempt to recuperate incommunicable perverse passions
within the symbolic, and an attempt to circumscribe and define the *"unknown relation"*?

Fetishism and all other perversions are libidinal ceremonies, utilizing certain objects as traces of, and instigations for, the passions. The fetish object is an apotropaic medallion that annuls the narcissistic wound. The fetishist loves details; such details escape iconography and are subsumed by the particular history of the subject, with all of its attendant accidents, errors, misinterpretations, and so forth.[17] If the icon arises from the symbolic, the detail develops from the passions, the imaginary. We might consider a particularly striking case, whose singularities suggest the possibility of a "hermeneutics of misreading" where the effects of libidinal oscillations are factored into the interpretative scheme as the feature of its very indeterminacy.

In *Confessions of a Mask* (1949),[18] Yukio Mishima recounts his first view of the reproduction of Guido Reni's *Saint Sebastian* (from the Palazzo Rosso in Genoa). "That day, the instant I looked upon the picture, my entire being trembled with some pagan joy." His very first orgasm soon followed, "bringing with it a blinding intoxication." The entire iconography of this depiction of a Christian martyrdom was of secondary import; rather, it was in the surprising sensuousness of the details that he reveled.

> The arrows have eaten into the tense, fragrant, youthful flesh and are about to consume his body from within with flames of supreme agony and ectasy. But there is no flowing blood, nor yet the host of arrows seen in other pictures of Sebastian's martyrdom. Instead, two lone arrows cast their tranquil and graceful shadows upon the smoothness of his skin, like the shadows of a bough falling upon a marble stairway.

Revealing a "strong flavour of paganism," this painting depicted "a remarkably handsome youth . . . bound naked to the trunk of a tree," exposing his "white and matchless nudity." He showed none of the decrepitude or suffering common to depictions of martyrdoms of the saints, but "only the springtime of youth, only light and beauty and pleasure"; rather than pain, his face and posture expressed "some flicker of melancholy pleasure like music."

This saint, whose mutilation—but never whose actual death and martyrdom—is depicted, is both the provocation and the sign of Mishima's passion. (Mishima was to pose for an infamous photographic depiction of Saint Sebastian, based on another work by Guido Reni from the Pinacoteca Capitolina in Rome.) In his particular, perverse inversion of the role of iconographic features and incidental details, the classic iconographic components of Guido Reni's painting are transformed into the least significant factors, while the details of Saint Sebastian's corporeal posture and ecstatic expression—free from iconographic restraint and thus different in each depiction—become the key features of Mishima's erotic appreciation of this artwork. It is the image's affective power, rather than its semiotic, communicative intent, that thrilled Mishima. And it is precisely the idiosyncratic nature of its effect that led him to conceive of what he termed a "confidential criticism," "a twilight genre between the night of confession and the daylight of criticism."[19]

The detail—be it iconographically significant or pure marginalia—is always susceptible to the libidinal oscillation between banality and overdetermination. Each recognition of yet another detail of a scene reorganizes the meaning of the entire scene: a painting is a diacritical system of signs where the meaning of each sign is fully dependent upon its relation to all the other signs, but where the meaning of the whole is a function of precisely which signs are taken as central by the hermeneutic process. The detail, that area of free play beyond iconographic restrictions, is both trope and trap. (In fact, the decorative is always significative: there are no purely "decorative" arts, opposed to the "fine" arts.) The detail's literal position is extremely tentative, fragile, since it can always be taken up as a term in the symbolic system of the picture, and thus play a figurative role; yet its symbolic position is equally delicate, since it may also be taken simply for what it denotes, a literal reading tempered by the iconographic context. (Hence the two limits of fascination: the epistemophilia of connoisseurship and the scoptophilia of fetishism—where, in the latter case, a libidinal reversal transforms iconophobia into iconophilia.) Ultimately, no detail can be fully gratuitous or marginal, as it is recuperated by the semiotic system of the painting. But this recuperation is a function of interpretation, and interpretation in turn is dependent upon the particular cathexes or decathexes of details within the viewer's libidinal economy. Semiotics contextualizes the detail; libidinal economy isolates the detail—or relegates it to oblivion. Criticism is founded upon the incommensurable exigencies of semiotic communicability and libidinal incommunicability: the detail may serve as the articulation of a scenario whereby the particular meaning of its iconography is fixed, or it may even serve as the very emblem of a cosmos[20]—or it may simply be isolated from the rest, and evoke no more or less than would the object that it depicts. How many traditions of criticism, and indeed how many metaphysics, rest upon these differences?

❖ ❖ ❖

The history of Western metaphysics entails the obfuscation, suppression, and indeed repression, of matter, chaos, the formless, the body. The tradition which subtends this current text originates in Nietzsche's desire to recuperate the body, and materiality itself, as the origin of philosophical speculation and the basis of all metaphysics: "Soul is only a word for something about the body. The body is a great reason."[21] This metaphysical reversal permits us to appreciate the profound importance, in the aesthetic register, of Gaston Bachelard's notion of a "muscular imagination."[22] The psyche is but the nominative sublimation of the body, of corporeal states and reactions. The imagination is but the ephemera of partial objects, the transgression by fragmentation of a cosmos all too unified and all too full to admit the particular, and peculiar, phantasms of our heretics of the spirit. Hence the transgressive character of Batille's observation that,

> In an arbitrary order where each element of self-consciousness escapes from the world (absorbed in the convulsive projection of the *self*), to the extent that philosophy, renouncing all hope of logical construction, arrives—as at an end—at a representation of relations

defined as improbable (and which are only the middle terms of the ultimate improbability), it is possible to represent this *self* in tears, or anxious. It can equally be thrown, in the case of a painful erotic choice, toward a *self* other than itself, but also other than any other.[23]

Witness, in this regard, the oneiric genesis of a woman in Proust's *Du côté de chez Swann* (1913):

> Occasionally, as Eve was born from Adam's rib, a woman was born in my sleep from the cramped position of my thigh. Formed from the pleasure that I was on the verge of tasting, I imagined that it was she who offered it to me. My body, which felt in hers my own warmth, wanted to unite with it; I awakened.[24]

Thus the projection of a world on the ego "surface" is both the ingression of an infinitude of "real," "objective" forms *and* the projection of phantasmatic forms, following the primary process logic of desire. And, following this "logic," we should not be surprised if our own dreams were to transform Eve into her libidinal double: Lilith.

In all but cases of the most extreme paranoia, identification is partial identification, just as all projection and introjection is partial, fragmentary, as dissociative as it is associative. Rational logic and visceral presence determine the polarities of the imagination, where conscious thought is always subverted by the monomania of the unconscious, where received opinion is always in conflict with perverse desire. Communicative structures of exchange *and* incommunicable phantasms; word *and* body; logos *and* corpus—without reduction or suppression, each must be granted its singular, though interrelated, existence. The "visceral imagination" suffers a double constraint: corporeal-gestural/semiotic-semantic. The libidinal/hermeneutic relationship is circular: since all libido is ultimately bound, it is "figured" by representational forms; but since all formal structures originate in and bear a libidinal charge, they continually serve as signs—however arcane—of the passions. Thus we must posit an aesthetics where theory and interpretation are juxtaposed to, or traced above, the effects of the passions, where a muscular contraction or spasm is worth as much as a concept.

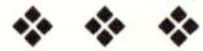

In the icon, intensity is fixed as symbol. (If we wish an ontotheological reading, *corpus* becomes *logos*—a short definition of sublimation.) Consider that extreme case of sublimation, always beyond the limits of representation: the sublime. The sublime is the absoluteness of exteriority, a counter-interiority, a counterintimacy. The (Kantian) sublime is the unrepresentable, the formless, that which cannot be grasped either in the unity of a single intuition or in its very principle. (It is a sort of desacralized stand-in for the infinitely perfect, distant, mechanical, and ultimately benign God of Spinoza, which replaced the representable, anthropomorphic God of the church fathers.) The sublime is the ultimate ontological ego-defense mechanism against narcissism and narcissistic wounds, the very dispossession of the origins of the self through a teleological repression. As Harold Bloom explains, the sublime is a mode in which the poet "is able to continue to defend himself against his own created image by disowning it, a defense of *un-naming* it rather than *naming* it."[25] As such, art, insofar as it aspires to the sublime, is, as Kurt Eissler claims, the "narcissistic projection of the destruction of narcissism.[26] Just as we can never recover the origins of the self, we can also never directly encounter the ultimate projection of the dissimulation of these origins, the sublime—only its symbols and indexes (but never its icons) appear. Thus, in Kant's famous example, the sight of a turbulent, violent sea (that ocean which he, in fact, never saw!) *evokes* the sublime, creating a sentiment of the terrifying, crushing reality that consumes our very being, invoking the insignificance of our contingent, material existence. The sublime manifests, on the aesthetic level, what Nietzsche called the tyranny of the absolute.

Yet it would be a mistake to consider the sublime as the prime aesthetic paradigm. We may contrast to this Bataille's notion of the *formless*: "On the other hand, to affirm that the universe resembles nothing and is only *formless* amounts to saying that the universe is something like a spider or spit."[27] For both Kant and Bataille, water, that archetypal symbolic floating signifier, delineates the limits of our comprehension. Yet, while the Kantian sublime marks our terror in regard to the ethereal and the infinite, the Bataillian countersublime marks our disgust with base materiality and the processes of the body. Sublimated desire turns us away from its objects; desublimation entails the rediscovery of such lost objects. The rarity of the heavens—and of the pure signified—is contrasted with the body's wastes. The sublime fascinates by escaping the gaze, beyond the limits of epistemophilia; desublimated base materiality captures the gaze in a fetishistic vortex of emotions, invoking a pronounced scoptophilia disengaged from ratiocination.

Sublimation—that system of substitutions, deflections, and deferrals of libido—serves as the metamorphosis of desire. Conversely, desublimation is the recuperation of libido, its recognition within the very forms of cultural artifacts (and artworks). Displacement of libido or replacement of libido; formation or deformation: the hermeneutic circle is not situated within a conflict of interpretations, but rather between sublimation and desublimation, between "civilizing" motivations and the barbaric avatars of Eros. Hermeneutic, interpretive judgments must be both universal, categorical, determinate, reactive, *and* singular, disjunctive, indefinite, active. As such, hermeneutics must be viewed in its intimate relation to all phantasmagoria—revealing, in Rosolato's terms, the very law-of-the-transgression-of-the-symbolic-law. (And, if this is indeed the case, then perhaps the current interest in the aesthetics of the sublime is merely a "retro" fashion: the "postmodern condition" would rather be discerned at that point where sublimation and desublimation intersect, or, as it appears on the stylistic level, collide.)

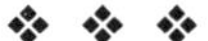

Sublime: a noun devoid of all denotation, sign of the absolute; a superlative adjective, restricted from all description; often a sheer interjection. Operating at that subtle juncture of nature and culture, the sublime is the projection of the most severe and discrete manifestations of the libido, the most terrifying and oppressive effects of the superego, and the most megalo-maniacal constructions of the ego. But isn't this all a tautology? Isn't every thought, affect, and object the result of the confluence of these psychic operations? If all the world is but a fable, if all is phantasmagoria, doesn't the sublime explain the limits of our phantasms, and the countersublime the limits of our bodies?

The classic differentiation between *libido vivendi, libido sentiendi, libido sciendi*—respectively, the desires to live, enjoy, know: the psychic functions of instinct, imagination, comprehension—is only a hermeneutic difference. The separation of these functions is just one connivance of the *libido sciendi* itself, to justify its own distinctness, to valorize sublimation, to dramatize (in both senses of the word, to stress and to stage) certain of the passions to the exclusion of the others. The major effect of the *libido sciendi* is that epistemophilia where the notion of the sublime transforms into sheer vanity those very objects of sublimation which are the real manifestations of our passions.

As scoptophilia is sublimated into epistemophilia in the quest for a *mathesis universalis*—where vision itself is quantified, transformed into words, numbers, axioms, formulas—iconophobia finally receives its logical confirmation. Doubtlessly, the development of a rationalist aesthetic and critical apparatus (as a cognitive supplement to the artwork) established the artwork's iconoclastic doubles: the text transforms the work of art into a figment, a fragment, of the imagination.

Yet there was a moment when iconophilia was indistinguishable from iconophobia. These curious relations were perhaps never more passionately (dispassionately?) revealed than in the work of Leonardo da Vinci, at that privileged historical moment just prior to the birth of a unified science and a rationalized aesthetic. Leonardo: "Lust is the cause of generation."[28] Yet this lust is nowhere evident in his work: consider the representations of the sexual act in his anatomical sketches. Expressionless faces, truncated or decapitated bodies drawn in cross section to reveal their internal forms, these works are notably devoid of lustfulness. (This is true to the point that one such sketch also reveals, as a marginal figure, a severed penis—an antilibidinal warning against whatever passions may be aroused by the scene of intercourse shown on the same sheet.) Indeed, it is precisely in regard to a primal cause of lust and generation—the female sex—that Leonardo's iconophilia and epistemophilia are tempered by a distinct iconophobia. The result is a gross distortion, a grotesquerie.

But we may fantasize these relations in a quite different manner. Consider the rapport between Leonardo's sketches of the actions and forms of flowing water and whirlpools and those fantastic depictions of cataclysmic, apocalyptic deluges which he produced toward the end of his life. And imagine a sketch of pubic hair—with the elegance and formal purity of a Praxiteles or a Michelangelo, depicting the fully stylized curls of hair in mathematical and pictorial similitude with the various movements of water—as the symbolic mediation between the whirlpools and the deluges. We would find the analysis of Eros and Thanatos into their component aspects. Thalassa mediates Eros and Thanatos: the origin of the world, in that pubic region de-eroticized and sublimated by Leonardo, is homologized with the catastrophic finale of the cosmic drama.[29] The end of the world meets its origin in a phantasmatic disaster where sublimation and desublimation intersect. The ultimate deformation and dematerialization of the world in the supreme, sublime manifestation of narcissism's desire to overcome its own wounds would proffer such a sketch of the pubis as an apotropaic emblem destined to abolish all fetishism. Here, a protoscientific epistemophilia (and iconophobia) would be in perfect equilibrium with an aesthetic scoptophilia (and iconophilia). But this is merely one long obsolete paradigm of the passions.

In Leonardo, the observed and depicted detail, escaping established iconography, creates an enigmatic, disquieting effect. Yet today, when there is no distance between the artwork and our deepest phantasms (a definition of modernism, perhaps?), the aesthetic icon could not be further from that foundational *logos* and *physis* dear to our philosophers (a foundation of iconoclasm, perhaps?). We must see in modernism—

abstract or otherwise—not a renewed iconophobia, but rather the final conjunction of iconophilia and the unconscious.

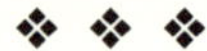

Courbet's *L'Origine du monde* (1866) is truly emblematic of origins: of art (witness the originary, paleolithic representations of the vulva); of modernism; and indeed, of the human world. It is also the origin of perversions. It reveals what the entire history of Western art—in fact, the entire history of the West all told—repressed: the invisible, unrepresentable female sex, veritable Medusa. And the fetish is our own personal fabulation of that repression, a substitute representation of that oxymoron, the absent female phallus. The fetish is a replacement for an absent sex or an absent God.

But once visible, this sight overturns our metaphysics, upsets our psychology, and reconstitutes our ethics. In *Madame Edwarda* (1937), Bataille raises this vision to its highest, yet most scandalous, indecent, blasphemous intensity. The narrator, encountering Madame Edwarda in her brothel, recounts:

> A voice, all too human, drew me out of my dazed condition. Madame Edwarda's voice, like her slender body, was obscene. "Do you want to see my old rags?" she said. Clutching the table with both hands, I turned toward her. Seated, she held one leg spread high in the air; to open her crack yet wider, she ended up drawing the skin apart with the fingers of both hands. Thus Madame Edwarda's "old rags" gaped at me, hairy and pink, as full of life as some repugnant octopus. "Why are you doing that?" I stammered weakly. "You see," she said, "I am GOD." "I'm going mad. . . . " "Oh no, you must look—look!" Her harsh voice softened and she became almost childlike in order to tell me with lassitude, with an infinite smile of abandon: "How I came!"[30]

In an origin all too human, the ontological and hermeneutic circles are complete; physical and metaphysical origins coincide; decadence and transcendence are one.

We may finally return to the phantasms of our novices, to realize that they just might be merely a slight textual supplement striving toward this unity of transcendence and immanence, a desire for the rare coincidence of an antinomian theology where desire regulates dogma—a theology whose heretical logic will doubtlessly escape their playful intentions. Their adoration, however, is a model not to be dismissed. We may conclude with a parallel but different adoration, at whose altar a very different love is manifested:

> After the death of an old American bachelor, a room 8 by 10 metres large, whose walls were lined with shelves, was discovered in his house in Passy. These shelves were covered with hundreds of assiduously cared-for shoes. In the middle of the room was a sort of prayer stool in beige calfskin. This salon, sheltered from the world, was kept locked up with a single key which only he possessed. Each afternoon he isolated himself there and spent three hours polishing dozens of pairs of shoes with the best wax. "It seemed to please Monsieur," explained his butler, "but he always emerged exhausted."[31]

2   compulsive beauty:
against surrealism

*In man creature and creator are united: in man there is material,
fragment, excess, clay, dirt, nonsense, chaos; but in man there is also
creator, form-giver, hammer hardness, spectator divinity and seventh
day: do you understand this contrast?*
—Friedrich Nietzsche, *Beyond Good and Evil* (#225)

What if we were to begin with a seldom cited phrase from Lautréamont's *Les chants de Maldoror*? "He is beautiful as the incertitude of the muscular movements in the folds of the soft parts of the posterior cervical region." Reflections on Surrealism have too long been captive of the influence of that other, now paradigmatic citation from Lautréamont, that cliché about the rapprochement of two distant realities: a sewing machine and an umbrella upon a dissecting table. What if the umbrella were to slowly grow fur and crawl away and the sewing machine transform itself into a hatrack, leaving us with a dissecting table upon which we can perform the required autopsies of a contemporary Forensic Theatre? What if we were to admit that the attempted reconciliation of Hegel and Freud in the hands of the Surrealists was in fact itself a surreal act, and hardly a coherent theoretical stance? What if our own serendipity were to lead us to a very different realm, perhaps a *subrealism*, inhabited by the refuse of our psyche and the detritus of our century?

There is, in fact, a double automatism at stake in Surrealism: an inner "psychic automatism" following the logic of the primary libidinal processes, a fortiori manifested in the dreamwork; and an external "objective chance" bowing to the causal exigencies of the cosmos. Whence the stylistic paradox of Surrealism: psychic and corporeal automatism lead to a rhythmic unity, an organic style manifesting biomorphic and anthropomorphic forms; to the contrary, objective chance permits the combination of *any* disparate forms whatsoever. The more distant the conjoined realities (whether psychic or physical), the greater the shock or fascination, the more surreal the result. Whence a key paradox: as there are no chance occurrences in the psychic mechanism (according to Freud) or in the historical dialectic (according to Hegel), Surrealist theory is but one more, albeit profound, version of realism, i.e., psychic realism. Surrealism certainly proffers a critique of modern, instrumental reality, which is constituted by the disavowal of desire: whence the necessity of creating a surreality which reveals, represents, and reinforces desire. And yet, there is neither reality nor surreality without the projection of the self—with its subsequent transformations and mutations—into the scene. The circle is vicious, and insidious: Surrealism discovers desire by representing the very mechanisms of repression which restrict the manifestations of desire in the social field, i.e., those psychic and social factors which create the ego to the detriment of the unconscious.

What, then, is Surrealism's originality? Might Surrealism not be a great art of psychic control, closely following the border between ego and libido? For if Surrealism is an oneiric art, we must remember that dreams are the results of repression, and most often stereotypically reveal a magma of everyday events. Whence the stylistic limits of Surrealism. Surrealist serendipity follows, in fact, a rather rigidly defined iconography, practically a stylistics, of what Breton termed an "interior model." Is this interior model that of the psychic mechanism in general, or is it rather limited by Breton's own mind?

Whence the iconographic limits, as well as the epistemological error, of Surrealism, a problem exemplified by the categorization of Surrealist objects: natural, interpreted natural, incorporated natural, perturbed, found, interpreted found, wild, mathematical, made, ready-made, aided ready-made, magic, and objects with a symbolic function. Were Surrealism rigorously Freudian (or Hegelian-Marxist, for that matter) it would have realized that all objects function symbolically, and that in fact the imagination constitutes a minor, if ever-shifting, site of the symbolic. For if, as Breton's epistemological nostalgia led him to believe, "the eye exists in a wild state," then everything must be aesthetically permitted. But that would lead us directly back to Dada, which had already outlived its first historical moment (to be reborn many times again, however, in other guises). Breton, in order to create the modernist myth that he so desired, had to suppress all that fell beneath the threshold of meaning. Like Freud, Breton was not only a dreamer, but also a policer and transformer of dreams: *nonsense* was the black beast of Surrealism, its suppressed core, its other.

Thus Breton had to impose limits. For example, Dali's acceptance of psychic automatism as pure iconographic license would permit him to depict not only scenes of definite surreal beauty, but also those of an equally surreal terror and kitsch. Given the exigencies of Surrealism—ethical, political, and aesthetic—such manifestations had to be contained. Yet if, as Breton insisted, our freedom is found in dreams, then we must also admit, following Dali, that our subjugation is found in nightmares. (Whence the fascination with Hitler as a manifestation of the demonic, by such figures as Bataille, Dali, Artaud.) The failure of Surrealist politics was a function of its aesthetics, caused by its restriction to a model of the individual psychic mechanism in an epoch wracked by collective passions.

A certain political trajectory is exemplified by three famous claims:

> Breton: "Beauty will be convulsive or it will no longer be."
> Dali: "Beauty will be edible or it will no longer be."
> Lettrist International collective: "The new beauty will be
> of SITUATION, that is to say *provisional* and lived."

The latter—a response by the Lettrist International collective (later to become the Situationist International, led by Guy Debord) to a 1954 Belgian Surrealist questionnaire—was the ultimate aesthetico-political contestation of Surrealism, one which would lead to the final disappearance of the art object, by transforming art into a form of agitprop. Henceforth, everyday life would become a work of art. For the future

Situationists, the beauty vaunted by Breton was not really convulsive enough, while Dali's was all too much so!

But the Surrealist project foundered not only upon the mass hysteria of the epoch's collective spirit: there was also an inner limit which could not be transgressed. After visiting the 1957 Redon retrospective at the Orangerie in Paris, Breton disclaimed the possibility of considering Redon a precursor of Surrealism. Speaking of the work of Redon, Breton wrote of his "horror, finally, of their pathological and larval quality." We can hear echoes of Breton's distaste for Bataille's celebration of the formless (the cosmos seen as a spider or a glob of spit), which is most comprehensible for someone who wished to remain a creator of forms. But we can only wonder about this fear of the pathological, expressed by the man who adored Nadja, celebrated *"l'amour fou,"* commemorated the fiftieth anniversary of hysteria with praise of Charcot's most famous patient, Augustine, and helped Dubuffet found the Compagnie de l'Art Brut. On the formal level, we could, of course, catalogue those artists in the Surrealist orbit whose formal concerns broached the larval: Tanguy's abstract biomorphisms and lithomorphisms; Ernst's "Histoire Naturelle," which abounds in monsters and mutations, and the incunabula of the imagination: Wölfli's mad drawings, whose motifs, scenes, texts, and simulacra of musical notation are constantly overrun by snails, birds, and sundry other obstacles to our comprehension. Breton's position was inconsistent: it would seem that the larval, the unformed, was variously experienced as either the source of new forms or the dangerous core of certain undesirable passions.

Perhaps nowhere has the larval played a more distressing role than in the drawings (not represented in Breton's collection) of Antonin Artaud, who was expelled from the Surrealist movement after having played a leading role in its formative years. These drawings, as Artaud explained, "are full of larval forms." In a text written after his release from the psychiatric asylum of Rodez, bearing the horrifying title of decomposition, "Dix ans que le langage est parti . . . " ("Ten years since language has departed . . . "), Artaud writes of his drawings:

What are they?
What do they signify?
The innate totem of man.
The amulets to return to man
All the breaths in the hollow
   gaunt
   pesti-ferous arcature
   of my true teeth.

Breton's "purely interior model" was a function of desire, guided by the pleasure principle; Artaud's "innate totems" were products of anguish, apotropaic talismans created to relieve him of the torments he suffered in the depths of his madness. Artaud's madness, as is generally the case with paranoia, entailed an implosion of reality (and, if one insists, of surreality) from which he could not escape. It was precisely this submersion in and struggle against psychotic deliria that permitted Artaud to eschew the "as if" quality of existence, to deny the efficacy of metaphoricity, to loath all iconicity in the presence of those powers, those forces, which wracked his body and soul. There is no argument, no logic, no theory here: only the admission of the exigencies of psychic force, of the libido, as it thrusts and is forever blocked in its sundry paths toward the unknown bliss of extinction. Artaud's now famous desire for a "body without organs"—announced in his radiophonic work, *Pour en finir avec le jugement de dieu*—was the ultimate anti-art, the ultimate anti-interiorizing passion. The body closed off in psychic refusal, reduced to its larval primacy. Not totem, but antitotem, his bowels to be cast out through his teeth on the airwaves of France. But this failed trajectory was, tragically, tangent with that of his own death.

Breton's own personal icon, his "totem" painting, was de Chirico's *Le cerveau de l'enfant* (1914; *The Child's Brain*), which he saw one day through the window of a bus, in a gallery window on the rue de la Boëtie. He was immediately compelled to stop and contemplate this pictorial enigma. This image—depicting a moustached man with his eyes closed, one arm hidden by a curtain, truncated at the waist by a table bearing a book—corresponds to the inaugural dream of Surrealism. For in *Les champs magnétiques*, written with Philippe Soupault, Breton recounts his dream where a sentence, with its corresponding image, knocked at his window one night: "There is a man cut in two by the window." Is this person Breton, the closed-eyed dreamer? Is it the father, truncated, castrated? Or must it remain enigmatic, as Surrealist protocol would insist? In any case, Breton acquired the painting and kept it until just before his death. In a sense, Breton's atelier, his collection of art and objects, was perhaps his greatest work, though not his most consistently Surrealist one. For his collection to have been truly Surrealist, it would have contained, side by side, *all* art; it would have corresponded to the epoch's other museological fantasy, Malraux's "museum without walls"; it would have been—like the work of God or of the unconscious—without any style whatsoever. Instead, it had a style, as did Surrealism in general: not that of "pure psychic automatism"—the limits of which Breton truly abhorred—but rather those of Breton's own taste, which was ultimately bourgeois: clean, healthy, that of an esthete opposed to all morbidity and perversion.

The Child's Brain was one of his collection's centerpieces. We can only be struck by the calmness of this "child's brain," by its highly interiorizing quality, and by its closure to the rest of the world. Nothing at all like the violence inherent in Lautréamont's very different ode to the brain: "beautiful as the incertitude of the muscular movements in the folds of the soft parts of the posterior cervical region." Perhaps, in final protest against any personalist, restricted, merely Bretonian model of Surrealism, we might end with the following remark, the following exorcism, of Henri Michaux, an early appreciator of Surrealism. In a different context, he proclaims, in *Difficultés* (1930): "The inner being continually combats gesticulating larvae. It suddenly finds itself emptied of them as of a scream, like detritus swept away by a sudden hurricane." Beneath all morphology we find the unformed, the imperfect: disfiguration and disincarnation haunt our works and our nights. Creature and creator, destroyer and destroyed, often exchange roles, unwittingly. Yet there is a difference, after all, between fearing the conquering worm and conquering the fearful worm.

3 innate totems:
artaud's drawings

He is this hole without frame that life wanted to enframe.
—Antonin Artaud, *"Le Retour d'Artaud, le Mômo"*

The art of seeing must be learned. Our gaze is stereotyped: we see according to visual and cognitive precedents. Art Brut and psychopathological art—especially the drawings and last texts of Artaud—serve as a disruption of our aesthetic domain, as the hidden side of the avant garde, sharing many of its effects while never directly confronting its worldly aspirations. Aesthetic information is a function of the relations between perceptual formations and artistic deformations of the visual field, regardless of where those disruptions arise. It is precisely within these interstitial cognitive gaps, these discursive slippages, these perceptual ruptures, that both sublimation and desublimation are effected. Works of Art Brut are evidence of these fractured manifestations of our souls. Perhaps the only way for us to truly reach the symbolic web at the core of these works is not through our criticism, but rather in the nightmares that they produce.

The aesthetic primacy of the body, as well as of the phantasms and deliria which the body creates, was never more forcefully manifested than in the work of Artaud. Consider his claim in "Manifeste en langage clair" (1925): "There is for me a certain evidence in the domain of the pure flesh, which has nothing at all to do with the evidence of reason. The eternal conflict between reason and the heart is settled within my very flesh, but this is a flesh irrigated by nerves."[1] These considerations go beyond the aesthetic; they bespeak an ethical imperative in regard to both the creative act and the appreciation of

39

the artwork. And they indicate the intense difficulties that underlie, and perhaps motivate, certain of these works. Pain, the memories of pain, or especially the overcoming of pain is transformed into meaningful signs of the relation of the artist's body to society—signs which we must take up as our own. According to Artaud: "I mean that there is in my drawings a sort of moral music, which I made by experiencing my brushstrokes not only through my hand, but also through the scraping of the breath of my cut-artery, through the teeth of my mastication" (21:266). Perhaps it is not coincidental that Jean Dubuffet began his collection of Art Brut at the very same moment that Artaud began to draw, in 1945. Dubuffet was the first person to visit Artaud in Rodez, where Artaud was being treated by Dr. Ferdière. And Ferdière certainly aided in inspiring the initial collection of Art Brut, as he shared some of his discoveries with Dubuffet.

Though not, strictly speaking, a creator of Art Brut—Artaud was an epitome of Western culture, through a sort of antagonistic, negative, demonic inversion—he was to be continuously excluded from the mainstream of modernist art. Artaud's career began and ended with rejection: for while Artaud was already excluded from the avant-garde art establishment by his break with Surrealism, he was even further cast "outside" the cultural realm by virtue of his extended period of incarceration in psychiatric hospitals. Whence his identification with Van Gogh, the man "suicided by society." Ultimately, Artaud's psychic state of appearing to be cast outside of his self—a manifestation of schizophrenic dissociation—can be read as emblematic of the manner in which this particular example of "outsiderness" was constituted.

In 1937, during a trip to Ireland, Artaud went mad. He was returned by force to France and spent the following nine years in various psychiatric institutions, notably at the asylum of Rodez, under the care of Dr. Ferdière, who treated him by a combinations of means, including electroshock and insulin shock therapy. Upon emerging from the nearly autistic depth of his malady, as well as surmounting the comalike effects of the shock therapies, he began to write numerous letters to friends, and in February 1945 he began to keep a journal, published as the *Cahiers de Rodez* (Vols. 15–21 of his *Complete Works*), which he worked on until his release in May 1946 and which were continued without interruption until the time of his death in March 1948 as the *Cahiers du Retour à Paris.*

If *The Theater and Its Double* was the manifesto of a theater of exorcism and curative magic as Artaud wished it to be, then this magic was never more needed than during his stay at Rodez. In his paranoid delusions, Artaud recognized that Satan was "that vacuity between me and my thought" (24:87), and that "God is the monomaniac of the unconscious" (15:315). He was caught in a web of conflicting identities bound by a schizophrenic megalomania, an ultimate dispossession of self. Here, the theological is subsumed within the pathological; the true prolegomena to any possible theater of cruelty, as well as perhaps its greatest manifestation, is the exorcism of God from the unconscious. This exorcism, this catharsis, was experienced in the form of a rebirth. "To die is to be done with God" (16:30). Many of his works of the period were created specifically as a defense mechanism against the treatment that he was receiving, as well as against the demons and God that tormented him; they are also the projection of the infinite intensity of his inner struggles.

> The goal of all these drawn and colored figures was the exorcism of a curse, a corporeal vituperation against the obligations of spatial form, of perspective, of measure, of equilibrium, of dimension, and through this demanding vituperation a condemnation of the psychic world incrusted like a crab-louse on the physique that it incubates or succubates by alleging to have formed it.

Yet Artaud was well aware not only of the necessary distinctions that must be made between his creations and art, but also between his works and the manifestations of psychopathological symptoms. In a letter to Dr. Ferdière, he writes: "You forget that I also staged theater, and that all of the stagings that I did were based upon a particular utilization of *psalmody* and of *incantation*."[3] Perhaps, but Artaud will also argue that it is equally not art.

> To the devil with art. There is not only art, there is the
> void, the abyss of what is always farther off, deeper, more
> absolute, which one day will be a being, not through per-
> fection or the absolute, but through this terrifying lack in
> being that is the driving characteristic of the persistence of
>
> puru purshe rasha shubane
> rasha shabune ara pursha
> rara rapuna tanu gada
> paha
> ketra terpuna aru kuda
>
> the infinite, which is not an idea but a being. (20:208–9)

And in *Van Gogh, le suicidé de la société*, he criticizes the psychiatric establishment: "You deem working consciousness delirium" (13:16), a critique which is furthered in his text
"Aliénation et magie noire" (Vol. 12). This active consciousness
is precisely what, for Artaud, is at the origin of his creativity,
while it is to the contrary a reactive consciousness—struggling
against shock therapies, abominable hospital conditions, iso-
lation, material privations, lack of recognition—that he believed exacerbated his madness.

Artaud began to draw in Switzerland in 1919, at the time
of his first stay in a psychiatric hospital (coincidentally, this was
both the moment and the locale of the height of the Dada
movement, as well as of the greatest Art Brut creator, Adolf
Wölfli, who was then painting in the Waldau asylum). He created numerous drawings at the asylum of Ville-Évrard in 1939,
conceived as magic objects to protect him against the imminent assassination that he feared. Yet his major production of
drawings began at Rodez and continued in Paris, culminating
with his illustrations for his book, *Artaud le Mômo* (1947) and
his exhibition of portraits in the Galerie Pierre (Paris, 1947).

Artaud's drawings—insofar as they serve as a magical
tool, an incantatory presence, a document of his inner condition, an expression of his desires, and a manifestation of his
life work—"definitively broke with art, style and talent."[4] Unlike his position in the theater, Artaud was untrained as a
painter. Consider his own descriptions of his techniques and

concerns; describing his drawing *La machine de l'être,* or *Dessin à regarder de traviole,* he explains:

> This drawing is a serious attempt to give life and exist-
> ence to what until today had never been accepted in art:
> the spoiling of the support, the pitiful clumsiness of forms
> which collapse around an idea after having toiled for so
> many eternities to be reunited with it. The page is dirtied
> and spoiled, the paper crumpled, the characters drawn as
> with a child's consciousness. (19:259)

Writing of the drawing *La maladresse sexuelle de Dieu:* "This drawing is voluntarily botched, thrown on the page as if in contempt for forms and features, so as to spurn the grasped idea and succeed in causing its fall." (20:173). And referring to his portraits: "These drawings must thus be accepted according to the barbarism and the disorder of their style of drawing, 'which is never preoccupied with art,' but with the sincerity and the spontaneity of the stroke."[5] His drawings are "full of larval forms" (14:77), which are a symbolic protest against the rules of aesthetic creativity and formalism.

> I mean that, knowing nothing of either drawing or of na-
> ture, I was resolved to leave behind forms, lines, outlines,
> shadows, colors, and views which, as they are used in
> modern painting, represent nothing, nor do they demand
> to be reunited according to the exigencies of any visual
> or material law whatsoever, but rather create on the pa-
> per a sort of counterfigure which would be a perpetual
> protest against the law of the created object.

Artaud continually argues that the force/form distinction in relation to his work is spurious—"I have only force and no ideas" (24:220)—a consideration at the very core of *Le théâtre et son double.* We find this notion already expressed in his correspondence with Jacques Rivière, an estimation which obtains, *mutatis mutandis,* for his drawings:

> This scatteredness of my poems, these defects of form, this
> constant sagging of my thought, must be attributed not
> to a lack of practice, a lack of command of the instrument
> that I employ, a lack of *intellectual development*; but to a

central collapse of the soul, a sort of erosion, both essential and fleeting, of thought. (1:28)

We might further explicate these issues by consideration of one of Artaud's major drawings, *L'exécration du Père-Mère,* created at Rodez in April 1945. In 1947 Artaud published a book of poetry entitled *Artaud le Mômo* (*Artaud the Madman*), which contained the poems: "Le Retour d'Artaud, le Mômo," "Centre-Mère et Patron-Minet," "Insulte à l'Inconditionné," "L'Exécration du Père-Mère," and "Aliénation et magie noire." The original project was to have the book illustrated by Picasso, but when Artaud was unable to obtain anything from him, he decided to illustrate it with his own drawings. He thus chose seven illustrated pages from his notebooks and one colored drawing, "L'Exécration du Père-Mère."

In order to gauge the unique and radical tone of these poems—which in turn will aid in establishing a context for understanding the drawings—a brief comparison might be made. In 1925 T. S. Eliot published his poem "The Hollow Men," at the very moment that Artaud edited the third volume of *La Révolution Surréaliste,* which had as its subtitle "1925: La fin de l'ère chrétienne," and which contained Artaud's scandalous attack, "Adresse au Pape." Eliot's wail of religious despair about the condition of modern humanity contains the famous lines:

> Between the desire
> And the spasm
> Between the poetry
> And the existence
> Between the essence
> And the descent
> Falls the Shadow
> *For Thine is the Kingdom.*[7]

Compare the following lines from "Le Retour d'Artaud, le Mômo" (the importance of which is indicated by the fact that there exist at least seven variants of this text contained in the dossier related to the book):

> Between the butt and the shirt,
> between the jism and the under-shove,
> between the member and the bad bounce,
> between the membrane and the blade,
> between the slat and the ceiling,
> between the sperm and the explosion,
> 'tween the fish-bone and 'tween the silt,
> between the butt and everyone's seizure,
> of the high-pressure trap
> of an ejaculation rattle
> is neither a point
> nor a stone (12:17)

Eliot's words are the despondent sign of belief within an increasingly godless world; Artaud's words proffer the sense of a struggle with a God about to be finally vanquished. Eliot's poetry is the epitome of language giving form to life; Artaud's work, and his life itself, is conceived as a radical struggle against form. Here is the difference between *the kingdom come* and *the kingdom overcome.* The paranoid religious conversion that Artaud underwent early on during his stay in psychiatric institutions was followed by a violent renunciation of the faith at Rodez; the *Cahiers de Rodez* are completely marked by this struggle, and all of his subsequent work, especially *Artaud le Mômo,* is written under the sign of his rejection of faith and his continual denunciation of God.

Artaud le Mômo is autobiography in its most virulent form. It poses the question:

> But what then in the end, you, the madman?
> Me?
> This tongue between four gums,
> this meat between two knees,
> this piece of hole
> for madmen. (12:14–15)

These holes, this void, this emptiness, this asshole, this cunt: such is precisely the image that he wants us to grasp, the sign that he places over his existence. Whence the monumentally iconoclastic aspect of his work. We find here the motivation for the genesis of the "body without organs" which appears in *Pour en finir avec le jugement de Dieu*. In "Interjections," the opening section of *Suppôts et supplications* (1946), there exists a total renunciation of existence expressed in a vast series of negations, including:

> no mind, no soul, no heart, no family, no families of be-ing, no legions, no confraternities, no participation, no communion of saints, no angels, no beings, no dialectic, no logic, no syllogistics, no ontology, no rule, no regula-tions, no law, no universe, no conception, no notion, no concepts, no affects, no tongue, no uvula, no glottis, no glands, no thyroid organs, no organs, no nerves, no veins, no bones[. . .] (14:13)

Here, the total negation of body and world heralds that extreme iconophobia which was to inform his drawings.

> And if you don't get the image,
> —and that is what I hear you saying
> in a circle,
> that you don't get the image
> which is at the bottom
> of my cunt hole.—
> it is because you don't know the bottom,
> not of things,
> but of my cunt. (12:16–17)

This text signifies the very "image" of nothingness, perhaps of death itself—it is the cataclysmic attempt to represent the unrepresentable. It may also, more specifically, describes the image whose title is identical to that of the second poem in the book: "L'Exécration du Père-Mère." For, further on in "Le Retour d'Artaud, le Mômo," he writes of himself as having been interred in the hole of the fireplace on the day he was killed:

> And afterward?
> Afterward?
> Afterward!
> He is this unframed hole
> that life wanted to frame.
> Because he is not a hole
> but a nose

> always a little too good at sniffing
> the wind of the apocalyptic
> head
> that one sucks on his clenched butt,
> and how good Artaud's butt is
> for pimps in Miserere. (12:19)

A distorted body, truncated at the waist; unidentifiable, partial body parts floating in a spaceless field; the sex covered by or replaced by a death's-head, surrounded by projectiles; machine-like instruments torturing the flesh, the "beef," the "meat," as Artaud says; an ethereal woman-like creature floating above it all—perhaps death incarnate. This is an archetypical expression of the experience of the fragmented, dismembered body—common to both dreams and schizophrenic states, where death and aggression are often the central themes. Jacques Lacan, in another context, explains:

> This fragmented body. . . usually manifests itself in dreams when the movement of the analysis encounters a certain level of aggressive disintegration in the individual. It then appears in the form of disjointed limbs, or of those organs represented in exoscopy, growing wings and taking up arms for intestinal persecutions—the very same that the visionary Hieronymus Bosch has fixed, for all time, in painting, in their ascent from the fifteenth century to the imaginary zenith of modern man. But this form is even tangibly revealed at the organic level, in the lines of fragilization that define the anatomy of fantasy, as exhibited in the schizoid and spasmodic symptoms of hysteria.

The *disjecta membra* of paranoid schizophrenic dissociation and projection are simultaneously a sign of the catastrophic effects of illness and the heroic egological attempts to reintegrate the psyche with reality. Yet while in Bosch and Breughal the pictorial disposition of these partial body parts and monstrous biomorphic inventions, these torments and terrors, is regulated and articulated by an arcane theological symbolism, in Artaud they are disarticulated through a megalomaniacal theological paranoia vanquished and turned upon itself. Yet once overcome, the persecutory destruction of the body is maintained and transformed into a symbol, a monument, to stand against such future persecution. Not only are these works antiformal and anti-aesthetic; they are even more so anti-institutional and anti-establishment.

It is in fact Artaud, and not Dubuffet, who can legitimately speak of an "asphyxiating culture" (the title of one of Dubuffet's books, written to express his anticultural position in the mythical year of 1968). Artaud's drawings were not only intended as a magical defense against the deaths inflicted upon him by electroshock therapy; they were later presented as a critique of, as a monument against, such therapy. Even more profoundly, they were the scream of a tormented spirit, in protest against the established order of the cosmos:

> . . . you will realize
> by my drawings, so awkward,
> yet so wily,
> and so shrewd,
> which say SHIT to this world.
> What are they?
> What do they signify?
> The innate totem of man.
> The amulets to return to man
> All the breaths in the hollow
>   gaunt
>   pesti-ferous arcature
> of my true teeth.
> Not one which isn't a breath expulsed in full force.

Most explicitly, there even exists in *Suppôts et supplications* a text entitled: *L'Homme et sa douleur: Commentaire d'un grand dessin fait à Rodez et donné au docteur Jacques Latrémolière pour le remercier de ses électro-chocs* (14:46–47). And in yet another letter from Rodez (4:1946), he writes of the drawing *La Mort et l'homme*—which depicts what might be a man receiving electroshocks, with a four-breasted woman, certainly Death herself, hovering in the foreground: "This drawing is a sensation that passed through me as certain legends recount that death passed." (21:232). Certainly, the forms manifested in these drawings are a function of the physical and social conditions of incarceration that Artaud suffered: the manifest content of schizophrenia, like the manifest content of dreams and neuroses, is dependent upon the subject's everyday experiences.

The rise of electrical technology has added new subject matter to these possibilities: electroshock apparatuses as torture devices; cinema, radio, telephone, and television as cosmic paranoid transmitters. While the psychic anxiety produced by paranoid "influencing machines" is perhaps not augmented by the creation of such new machines, the physical pain produced by new forms of medical treatment was indeed increased. All these new forms (of treatment, of torture, of cure) are often relived within a theological system of deliria, since the hyperbolic, absolute nature of religious experience is the ideal foil for megalomaniacal paranoid projections. However, the profound content of these works is definitively unrepresentable: pain. Whence the destruction of icons and their double, the body.

4   pressures of the sun: manifesto against the electric drug

State of nerves, states of mind, state of the world. There are moments when the universe seems to resemble most closely a scalp quivering with electric jolts.

—Antonin Artaud, *Letters to Génica Athanasiou*

" . . . the liver is the filter of the unconscious, while the spleen is the physical guarantor of the infinite."[1] Flesh has never been as tormented, a soul has never been as bewitched, a voice has never been so threatened. Addicted to opiates early in life, Artaud's liver and spleen were both saturated with an artificial paradise, much more so than his spirit was enamored of Baudelaire. The unconscious was skewed, infinity foreshortened, nerves frayed. "Imagine that I now physically feel the passage of this volition, imagine that it jolts me with a sudden and unexpected electric shock, a repeated electric shock" (1:43). Only by overcoming the difference between force and form—the very rupture at the base of metaphysics—can the essence of life be attained, that "fragile and fluctuating core untouched by forms" (4:18). Here the myth of force takes on a twentieth-century dimension: the dynamo and the virgin vie for contact with the nervous system that constitutes the soul.

The soul is something of the body; God is the manifestation of organic secretions; grammatical reflexivity returns speech to its corporeal origins; thought is shaken to its core by a foreign volition, by "sudden and unforeseen electricity" (1:43). Theater, the theater of cruelty, will touch the marrow, or it shall no longer exist. Theater as surgery (2:22). "The theater is an exorcism, a summoning of energy . . . it must abandon individual psychology, enter into mass passions, into the conditions of the collective spirit, grasp the collective wave-lengths" (5:153). Theater as paroxysm. Indeed, a lifetime of opiates (and their moralistic pharmacological inversion, bismuth cures) hardly sufficed—a certain homeopathy, a curative magic, was necessary. Perhaps the theater would reach deeper, "like a bath of psychic electricity in which the intellect would be periodically reimmersed" (4:321).

Obsessed by the idea of Mexico, a baroque Mexico, volcanic earth, Indian blood, magical realities, chimerical visions, a culture of fire, of the sun. An ancient solar culture founded on the supremacy of death, where destruction is a precondition of rebirth and transformation (8:269). Everything already hieratic, already cruel. Such is the immemorial Indian culture that burns organisms, boils the blood, irrigates the nerves: "The civilization of Mexico lives on a nightmare of organs" (8:159), writes Artaud, echoing "the limbo of a nightmare of bones and muscles" (1:117) which characterized his own existence in *Fragments of a Diary from Hell* (1926). Even before his departure, Artaud's Mexico was bound by the clichés of his own partially ecstatic, partially pathological, partially visionary phantasms. This inner Mexico was a fertile nervous illumination or stimulation, strangely resembling Artaud's impossible theater of cruelty. It was in the land of the Tarahumaras that Artaud discovered, or intuited, a scenario that coincided with his desires: the rite of Tutuguri. To reach this land, Artaud—having discarded the last of his opiates, thus being without narcotics for the first time in seventeen years—traversed a forest of signs, bewitched. The mountains revealed hallucinated figures of men tortured by gods, among which nature capriciously disclosed the image of a nude man nailed to the rocks and tortured under a volatilized sun—Artaud crucified at Golgotha (9:219), Artaud burnt at the stake (9:62). Beside every road sprouted a burnt tree in the form of a cross or of strange beings—signs that he was approaching his goal (9:44–47).

Artaud habitually inscribed his name into his works: in *The Theater and Its Double* the ship that bore the plague to Marseille was named the "Grand-Saint-Antoine" (4:20); in *Henchmen and Supplications* the nomination is disarticulated: "AR-TAU, where they always wanted to see the designation of a dark force, but never that of an individual" (14:147). Artaud's autobiography is an account of various transpositions of the personal into the sacred, across time and space: God is transformed into paranoid torments and psychic catastrophes, where God and the Devil are one, and where Tutuguri is confused with Christ (9:103*ff*); and the ultimate desire is to void the unconscious of the God that perpetually and monomaniacally tormented him.

Tarahumaras. Tutuguri. Ciguri. Were these names, for Artaud, any less rich than the glossolalia that punctuated his years of madness and his last writings?

> o dedi
> a dada orzoura
> o dou zoura
> a dada skizi
>
> o kaya
> o kaya pontoura
> o ponoura
> a pena
> poni (12:13)

In *The Theater and Its Double*, Artaud insisted that the theater of cruelty must function as a sort of curative magic, where language will be manifested in the form of incantation (4:56). In Mexico he sought one of the last places on earth where the curative peyote dance still existed, a festival that would liberate his body and illuminate his inner landscape. To reach the land of the Tarahumaras, Artaud experienced twenty-eight days of arduous and hallucinatory journey, symptoms of drug withdrawal, psychic turbulence, vast expectations; he was reduced to "a heap of poorly assembled organs" (9:50).

His trajectory led him through a Tarahumara village dominated by giant decorated phalli (9:125), which couldn't but cause him to recollect his own tale of that other solar god, Heliogabalus, and of the colossal ten-ton stone phallus that preceded this emperor's triumphal march into Rome. The sun is the most generalized manifestation of energy, of force *contra* form, a sign of eternity, of God. Artaud would write in

Heliogabalus of this Emperor-God as "son of the summits, false Antonin, Sardanapalus, and finally Heliogabalus, a name that seems to be the auspicious grammatical contraction of the highest denominations of the sun" (7:14). Antonin Artaud would inscribe his name in this solar theology, celebrating the false Antonin as a sun-god who is the very principal of anarchy, the breath of chaos itself, a breath which would pierce the body and excite the nerves. "The erectile member is the sun, the cone of reproduction on earth, as Heliogabalus, sun of the earth, is the cone of reproduction in the heavens" (7:81). *Heliogabalus* begins: "Just as there was an intense circulation of blood and excrement around Heliogabalus' corpse, dead without a tomb, his throat cut by his own police in the latrines of his palace, there was around his cradle an intense circulation of sperm" (7:13). This scatological characterization is later echoed in *The Tarahumaras,* where the sorcerer speaking of the Ciguri explains that the realm of appearances presents itself as "the obscene mask of he who sneers between sperm and caca" (9:31).

Artaud finally participated in the rite of Ciguri, the rite of Tutuguri, led by the priests of the sun acting as manifestations of the word of God. (This heretical, abject Catholicism existed in both the Tarahumara-Catholic syncretism and the inner schismatism of Artaud's phantasms.) Ciguri isn't simply peyote, but rather the god himself who enters one's nerves; Ciguri is infinity (9:24). The therapeutic action of this remedy depends on the total pillaging of our organism; Ciguri is man himself assassinated by God (9:27). This devastating metaphysical homeopathy is desublimated by Artaud into anti-cultural poetics (8:267).

The ritual dance takes place on sacred ground: a pyre surrounded by a circle traced on the ground, upon which are ranged ten crosses of unequal height, each bearing a mirror. As the sun sets, the sorcerers enter the circle and dance, possessed, as if epileptic, chanting, whirling, their heads deformed by the mirrors, swelling and disappearing in the flames of the pyre (9:60)—as in *The Theater and Its Double,* where, to counter the aesthetic fascination with forms, actors must become as "victims burnt at the stake, signalling through the flames" (4:18). But the truth of the rite is not expressed by external forms; rather, an inner transformation, aided by the psychopharmaceutical effects of peyote, changes consciousness, activating the marvelous, the fantastic, and producing visions of God. "What emerged from my spleen or from my liver had the form of the letters of a very ancient and mysterious alphabet masticated by an enormous mouth, yet horrendously choked, proud, *illegible*, jealous of its invisibility" (9:32–33). The incantations of the Tarahumaras and the glossolalia of Artaud's madness merged and were hypostatized.

> rai da kanka da kum
> a kum da na kum vönoh (9:117)

But this vision was followed by another, in which the spleen was transformed into an immense emptiness, an oceanic void upon which a fire-sprouting root was stranded. This was the root of the peyote plant, the root of Ciguri, made one with self and world. The unconscious is a language; the cosmos is nothingness. As things returned to normal, Artaud didn't know whether it was he himself or the world that had fainted. Regardless, he had seen the spirit of Tutuguri.

His written reflections on these visions end proleptically with the admission of yet other, false and excruciating, perceptions and sensations which he suffered while incarcerated in the psychiatric hospital of Rodez during the summer of 1943, the very year in which this chapter of *The Tarahumaras* was written. They bespeak the electroshock treatment which he endured there. He saw himself encircled by demons, which he tried to fend off by making the sign of the cross or by written and chanted incantations. "I also wrote, on any available scrap of paper or on the books I had in my possession, conjurations which had little value either from a literary or a magical point of view, since things written in this state are no more than the residue, the deformation or rather the counterfeiting of the lofty lights of LIFE" (9:35–36). Insisting that Lewis Carroll's poem "Jabberwocky" was in fact a plagiarism of one of his own long lost works entitled *Letura d'Eprahi Falli Tetar Fendi*

Photia o Fotre Indi, he offered his publisher (in a letter from Rodez in 1945) the following sample of how a translation of the former should appear:

ratara ratara ratara
atara tatara rana

otara otara katara
otara ratara kana

ortura ortura konara
kokona kokona koma

kurbura kurbura kurbura
kurbata kurbata keyna

pesti anti pestantum putara
pest anti pestantum putra (9:188)

A curse upon the rotten plague, a curse upon medically inflicted comas, a curse upon his wretched, shocked body. As with the rite of Ciguri, religious mania manifested itself as a struggle, one now magnified by paranoid deliria—a paranoia based in part on what he suffered at the hands of his doctors.

In a postscript, we are informed that he wrote "The Rite of Peyote" in a state of religious conversion, after having swallowed between 150 and 200 hosts. No longer a theological homeopathy, this eucharistic overdose was part of a christological delirium, now syncretized, briefly, with Tarahumara theology. Yet Artaud seems to have ultimately won his struggle with God at Rodez: his vehement imprecations against his baptism bespeak a break with God and his minions—angelic, diabolic, and priestly. He also informs us in this postscript that, "there is nothing more erotically pornographic than the christ, ignoble sexual concretization of all false psychic enigmas," concluding that his "basest acts of masturbatory magic engage the electric prison release" (9:40).

Laudenum, bismuth, peyote, eucharistic wafers: at Rodez a new drug was utilized, the electric drug. Electroshock therapy—which passes a 200-volt current of between 5 and 250 milliamperes through the body for between one-tenth and one-half second—causes violent epileptoid seizures and a conse-

quent coma, often resulting in loss of memory of the shock itself. This procedure was conceived by Hugo Cerletti in 1938,
after having visited the abattoirs of Rome, where the animals
were put in a state of shock before being slaughtered. Artaud
suffered this avant-garde cure which caused both real and
symbolic wounds, resulting in what he protested as being an
"artificial death" (12:60). As Artaud declaims in "Alienation
and Black Magic" (broadcast over French radio in July 1946,
just after his release from Rodez), psychiatric hospitals are re-
positories of black magic, a magic based on modern therapeutic techniques such as insulin shock and electroshock, which
he renames BARDO. "Bardo is the death throes that reduce the
self to a puddle" (12:58). Such "electrical introspection," he explains, is akin to "the spitting of the stalk" (*le crachat de la râpe*),
part of the Tarahumara rituals. Like the rite of Ciguri, there
are theological consequences: electroshock "kills Artaud and
makes God return" (20:53). Thus it is appropriate that "The
Rite of Peyote" ends with a discussion of electroshock and conversely that his last works evoke Mexico. "Alienation and
Black Magic" concludes:

> farfadi
> ta azor
> tau ela
> auela
> a
> tara
> ila (12.60)

It too is followed by a postscript, written just a month before
his death, indicating that a blank page should be placed between the text and all the squirmings of Bardo which appear
in the limbo of electroshock. In this purgatory, this borderland
of lost souls, a special typography should be used to heighten
certain verbal effects, specifically in order "to abject god"
(12:61).

One of the texts that was to have been part of Artaud's
radiophonic broadcast *To Have Done with the Judgment of God*
(1948) was entitled "The Theater of Cruelty." It opens with
the greatest scatological abjecting of God: "Do you know of

anything more outrageously fecal than the history of god and of his being: SATAN" (13:107). Earlier in this work, in the section entitled "In Search of Fecality," he insists that man has sacrificed his blood because he desires shit:

> o reche modo
> to edire
> di za
> tau dari
> do padera coco (13:84)

In yet another section of this work, "Tutuguri: Rite of the Black Sun," the earlier Christian-Tarahumara syncretism is reversed and abolished, in the desire to have done with the judgment of God. Writing anew of the rite of Ciguri, Artaud exclaims: "The major tone of the Rite is precisely THE ABOLITION OF THE CROSS" (13:79). This first version of Artaud's "Tutuguri" was followed by a second, completed two weeks before his death. It begins: "Created for the external glory of the sun, *Tutuguri* is a black rite. The rite of the black night and of the *eternal* death of the sun. No, the sun shall no longer return" (9:70). This apocalyptic text was a return to Mexico, now and always the phantasmatic projection of an inner conflict. In "The Theater of Cruelty," the guiding metaphor is no longer the sun: "The human body is an electric battery whose discharges have been castrated and repressed, whose capacities and emphases have been oriented toward sexual life, while in fact it was created precisely in order to absorb, by its voltaic displacements, all the stray reserves of the infinite void" (13:108).

To Have Done with the Judgment of God was to have been Artaud's major late work, if its broadcast had not be suppressed at the last moment, due to its scandalous, blasphemous nature. Artaud (who apparently played Fantômas on the radio earlier in his life) risked his final work on the transmitting capabilities of modern media. Radio, like the plague, would directly attack the nervous system of the socius. Perhaps he also realized the futility, or at least the unwieldiness, of the thousands upon thousands of pages of diaries he wrote at Rodez and Paris; perhaps he thought that their essence could be condensed into a single recording, which could then be played back at will, even during sleep, so that his deliria would then reenter consciousness, transformed into the crystalline Apollonian coldness of dreams.

Yet there were also inner psychic risks. In sound recording, the organic rhythms of the body are reified and ultimately destroyed by electromechanical reproduction, only to be returned by artificial means. Thus sound recording produces a theft and transformation of the voice, an alienation of the self in a mind/body split, with its consequent quotient of anguish. In such a split the hypostatization of Cartesian metaphysics or the manifestation of psychopathology? The mind is no longer neatly attached to the body by means of the pineal gland, as Descartes insisted; thought is now pandemonium, (literally, the abode of all demons).

The psychiatric asylum may be deemed a representational, theatrical system, one which is particularly closed—as closed as the psychoses that breed within its confines. The asylum is thus a prosthesis of that other scene, the unconscious, always suppressed from public view. Compare the recording studio. While the radio broadcasts and thus externalizes the voice, the asylum interiorizes it, causing an impacting, an aggression of the voice within the body, within consciousness, within the unconscious. In electroshock therapy, the subject is wired; in radiophonic art, the subject is wireless, The dynamo replaces the virgin, electricity replaces the sun, schizophonica replaces schizophrenia, and potentially paranoid machines are directed outward to shock others, the listeners. Telephone, cinema, radio, television: parallel communication and representational systems exist as alternative prosthetic devices, lures, and prisons for our fears and passions.

We see here the paradox, and the tragedy, of *To Have Done with the Judgment of God*: this unbroadcast broadcast, this antirepresentational representation, this fixed spontaneity was repressed and transfigured according to the political, historical, and technical exigencies of the radiophonic art. Did Artaud ultimately have done with the judgment of God, or did God finally prevail in the end, stealing Artaud's voice yet again—

this time not to have the spirit descend into a body wracked with pain and speaking in tongues, but rather to severe voice from body, transforming the voice into an object and casting it into the world, where it was doomed to be lost on the airwaves, or in the archives? In a letter to Paule Thévenin written just before his death, Artaud explains that henceforth he will create only for the theater, never again for the radio: "Where there is the *machine* there is always nothingness and the abyss; there exists a technical intervention that deforms and annihiliates all that one has done" (13:146).

Machines had always plagued Antonin Artaud. At the age of five Artaud began to suffer those terribly debilitating headaches which were to plague him for the rest of his life. He had contracted meningitis and risked imminent death. In desperation, his father attempted a therapy quite in vogue at the time: he purchased a huge machine that produced static electricity. As the air filled with ozone, electric sparks arced from its wires to an electrode attached to the young patient's head . . .

5 between the desire and the
spasm: a libidinal aesthetics

A rt must be erotic and contentious, or it shall no longer be. Written in the current political climate—where the fear, censorship, and repression of eroticism are once again prime factors in cultural politics—it is hoped that this brief essay may offer some avenues for analysis and polemic. For in an epoch where Eros is being transformed into a demonic myth, and erotic joy presented as a dystopian ideal, a certain practice and discourse—be it critical, theoretical, or fictional— must remain in opposition.

The post-1968 French aesthetic discourse on eroticism may be traced back to two disparate but seminal [*sic*] events that took place in 1946–47: Antonin Artaud wrote and recorded his infamous radiophonic work, *Pour en finir avec le jugement de Dieu;* and Marcel Duchamp, his last major work, *Étant Donnés:1° La chute d'eau, 2° Le gaz d'éclairage.* The former was not broadcast on French radio until the 1970s; the latter was revealed only upon Duchamp's death in 1968, when it was presented to the Philadelphia Museum of Art.

Contemporary French aesthetic theory, as well as the discourse on eroticism, is profoundly marked by a reaction against the previously dominant aesthetic position of Surrealism. In contrast to Breton's bourgeois aestheticization, the figures with whose influence we shall be dealing in this text— Debord, Duchamp, Artaud—all produced what may be deemed counteraesthetics, if not anti-aesthetics. While the source of this polemic may be traced back to the ruptures in the Surrealist movement between 1927 and 1930 instigated by the expulsions of Artaud, Bataille, Masson, and Leiris, our present task will be to trace out this problematic in regard to that other major rupture in the French cultural scene: the events of May 1968. The connection between these two moments is profound, and their respective polemics often assume the same rhetorical forms.[1]

The politicization of art was already intense in *Surréalisme au service de la révolution,* published in the late 1920s, and then further augmented under the Front Populaire in the 1930s. It reached its culmination in the Lettrist International, later to become Situationism. The Lettrist International slogan that "Beauty, *when it is not a promise of happiness,* must be destroyed," may be considered paradigmatic of the radical politicization of art at the core of May 1968 counteraesthetics.[2] This sentiment is at the origin of such May 1968 graffiti as: "Art is dead. Let us create our daily lives." The liberatory political aspirations of Situationism would eliminate the artwork by transforming the aesthetic act into a mode of utopian agitprop.

Situationism's theoretical position is based on the premise that "The spectacle is not an ensemble of images, but a social relation between people, mediated by images."[3] As a self-portrait of power, the spectacle is analyzed as being "capital at such a degree of accumulation that it becomes image."[4] This implies the alienation of work and social existence, false consciousness of time, falsification of appearances, banalization of discourse, and the paralysis of memory and history. To counter these social ills, Situationist aesthetics endeavored to transfigure spectatorship itself. The fragmentary, collage aspects of its works cannot be considered as a new style, but rather as an antiformalism, where cognitive articulations are established by the spectator, not the artwork.

Situationist activism was conceived as antispectacle. Rather than being an artist or cinematographer, the Situationist would be a "director of situations."[5] This was achieved by *détournement,* the diversion or misappropriation of found materials (an old Dadaist and Surrealist ploy). This position is the hyperbolic manifestation of politicized aesthetics: art become "situation" implies, if not the total loss of the art object, at least its ephemeral, anticommodity existence. It entails the transition from a solitary, idealizing "utopian revolutionary art" to a collective "experimental revolutionary art."[6] This is art as revolutionary propaganda, with the intent of shattering the false consciousness and false coherence of the real. These positions would transform the isolated Situationist group into one of the central actors of the events of May 1968, where political liberation implied an erotic liberation that would have its theoretical and practical effects on subsequent artistic practice.

The theoretical conditions made possible by Situationist activism intersected with the earlier postwar French leftist political-philosophical aspirations of the existential phenomenologists, notably Sartre and Merleau-Ponty. The writings of the latter were central to the post-1968 discourse on eroticism. Merleau-Ponty's key aesthetic statement, "Eye and Mind," proffers a phenomenological epistemology and ontology in which the corporeal paradigm predominates: "Everything I see . . . is marked upon the map of the 'I can.' . . . The visible world and the world of my motor projects are each total parts of the same Being."[7] The body is lived as "that strange object which uses its parts as a general system of symbols for the world."[8] Thought is neither pure conceptuality nor an ideal signification, but rather a function of the lived, eroticized, contingent, situated, historicized body. In terms of sexuality proper, Merleau-Ponty specifies in *Phenomenology of Perception*:

> Sexuality conceals itself from itself beneath a mask of generality, and continually tries to escape from the tension and drama which it sets up. . . . Sexuality is neither transcended in human life nor shows up at its center by unconscious representations. It is at all times present there like an atmosphere. . . . Sexuality becomes diffused in images which derive from it only certain typical relationships, only a certain general emotional physiognomy. . . . Sexuality, without being the object of any intended act of consciousness, can underlie and guide specified forms of my experience.[9]

Merleau-Ponty's ultimate, unfinished work, *The Visible and the Invisible*, proposes a new ontology based upon his reflections about the "flesh," hitherto unexpressed in any philosophy. The flesh is not the substance of the body, but rather the manner in which the body is intertwined with the world, with others, and with itself; it expresses the "narcissism of vision" at the very core of visibility; it is, like the pre-Socratic notion of the elemental, the manner in which the world becomes world for us. Our adhesion to being, to the flesh, is a mode of investment (*investissement; Besetzung*), whereby desire and conceptuality are inextricably united in the formation of meaning and praxis. The Cartesian ego, as well as all transcendental forms, disappears within this decentered, fragmented ontology.

Criticizing the mechanistic, causal understanding of the unconscious in Freudian metapsychology, Merleau-Ponty explains: "Hence what Freud wants to indicate are not chains of causality; it is, on the basis of a polymorphism or amorphism, what is contact with Being in promiscuity, in transitivism, the fixation of a character by investment of the openness of Being in an entity."[10] This libidinal, energetic model of the psyche is paralleled by the aesthetic notion of the painted line as a disequilibrious, modulating, corporeal trace. It is precisely painting which expresses the very origins and proffers the very articulations of lived, eroticized spatiality. "Painting awakens and carries to its highest pitch a delirium which is vision itself."[11] The painting is not a mere object or representation, but rather a mode of visibility; it is something we do not simply see, but rather something according to which we see, feel, understand. Merleau-Ponty explains:

> It is Matisse who taught us to see their contours not in a "physical-optical" way but rather as structural filaments, as the axes of a corporeal system of activity and passivity. Figurative or not, the line is no longer a thing or an imitation of a thing. It is a certain disequilibrium . . . the restriction, segregation, or modulation of a pre-given spatiality.[12]

This corporeal ontology and aesthetics, motivated by libidinal investment, was taken upon by Jean-François Lyotard:

> Why and how is there a *capture* and *inscription* of this wandering energy in a formation or figure? *Why?* Because everything that is given as an object (thing, painting, text, body . . .) is a *product*, that is to say, a result of the meta-

morphosis of this energy from one form into other forms. Each object is energy at *rest*, quiescent, provisionally *conserved, inscribed.* The apparatus or figure is only a *metaphoric operator.* It is *itself* composed of stabilized and conserved energy. Freud employs the word *investment* in this sense.[13]

Inspired by the analysis and rhetoric of Nietzsche's aesthetic rift between the Dionysian and the Apollonian as expressed in *Twilight of the Idols* ("Toward a Psychology of the Artist"), Lyotard explains in *Discours, figure* that "beneath the figural is difference, not simply the trace . . . but the primary process, the principle of disorder, the impulsion toward joy; not any interval whatsoever separating two terms of the same order, but an absolute rupture of equilibrium between an order and a non-order."[14] Lyotard's *Économie libidinale* begins with a description of the flayed body as an "opening up of the libidinal surface," such that the entire body, inside and out, is grasped as a potentially libidinal mechanism.[15] Here, the human skin exists as a passage of intensities; and in an epistemological/ hermeneutic conundrum, his book itself is deemed a fragment produced by a certain flux of such intensities. As such, all culture exists as a function of the psychic primary processes. This position was certainly influenced by Roland Barthes's *Le plaisir du texte,* published a year earlier, which calls for the institution of a *poesis singularis* in contradistinction to the positivist Cartesian method and ideal of a *mathesis universalis;* and also perhaps by Gaston Bachelard's phenomenological notion of the primacy of a "muscular imagination," as revealed in his *Lautréamont.*

Lyotard's earlier work, *Discours, figure,* is a summation of contemporary metapsychology, structural linguistics, and phenomenological aesthetics written contemporaneously with the events of May 1968. *Discours, figure* proposes a specifically aesthetic study of libidinal effects, where he stresses that "This book is a defense of the eye, of its localization." This study of the libidinal constitution of all vision reveals the eye as a force, as a libidinal mechanism; aesthetics becomes a matter of charting the cathexes, decathexes, and countercathexes of the libidinal economy. Painting is thus a libidinal apparatus, ruled by an "energy susceptible to transformations and metamorphoses."[16] The body's inherent polymorphism and heterogeneity is thematized in the artwork: Bellmer's *poupée,* for example, entails, "the de-localization of energy by its re-localization elsewhere (energy abounds in the tooth: there is then its displacement and focalization upon another region, for example the palm). This is an energetic apparatus, an operative transformer, in this case a transformer of a single locality of energy."[17] Within the intertwining of figure and discourse, the eye is deemed to be at the very core of all discourse; conversely and concurrently, discourse serves as the grid according to which vision is constituted. As such, the aesthetic domain is ruled by three "fundamental modes of connivance that desire links to figurality: the transgression of the object, the transgression of form, the transgression of space."[18] This aesthetic theory, which is intimately informed by Nietzsche's and Bataille's models of transgressive eroticism, is an energetics, specifically oriented against Lacan's structuralist, semiological aesthetics, where desire is deemed to be ruled by a lack, rather than being a productive source. Lyotard's aesthetic libidinal economy will later be fully worked out in regard to a single *oeuvre* in his *Les transformateurs Duchamp.*

Such an anti-Lacanian, antisemiological, and antimetaphysical celebration of disequilibrium, of non-order, of rupture, and of *jouissance*, is brought to its epistemological and rhetorical limits in Gilles Deleuze and Félix Guattari's *Anti-Oedipe* and *Mille Plateaux.* The antimetaphysical thrust of these works, and indeed of Deleuze's entire *oeuvre*, may be schematized by the following dichotomies, in which the first term of each division is always valorized: rhizomatic/arborescent, nomadic/sedentary, chaos/cosmos, chance/necessity, difference/identity, detotalizing/totalizing, active/reactive, schizophrenic/paranoid, anti-oedipal/oedipal, anarchic/hierarchic, desire/repression, deterritorialization/territorialization, polymorphous-perversity/genitality. As all ideality, essentiality, and transcendence are rooted to facticity, philosophy must henceforth become a productive, and not a descriptive, discipline: a manifestation of desire. Henceforth, any logic must be of the particular, and not of the universal: a logic of events. Henceforth, thought must be ruled by the rhizomatic combination of signifiers: an anarchic manner of distributing attributes.[19]

Anti-Oedipe marked a culmination of the post-1968 theoretical celebration of desire. The central thesis is that desire itself produces reality, such that, in effect, no difference exists between the production of desire and social production.[20] This work parallels Lyotard's contemporaneous analyses in *Discours, figure* (hailed by Deleuze and Guattari as the first generalized critique of the signifier, which is overtaken by the figural) and *Économie libidinale,* where the fundamental basis of human existence is seen to be the flow and stoppage of pure libidinal intensities. These analyses permit the establishment of an aesthetics of production and not representation.

The diagnosis of this "desiring-production" is based upon the paradigm of schizoanalysis, i.e., an anti-Oedipal, antineurotic, antiparanoid, heterogeneous realm of theoretical activity that surpasses the gestaltist limitation of traditional models of epistemology. No longer based upon the conjunctive distribution of predicates and attributes at the core of metaphysics from Aristotle through Kant and Hegel, such schizoanalysis reveals disjunctive signifying chains void of any central schema: "These chains are the locus of continual detachments—schizzes on every hand that are valuable in and of themselves and above all must not be filled in."[21] Libidinal flows must be understood as fragmented, detached from the despotic Oedipal signifiers that attempt to rule them through an insidious micropolitics of control that functions, first and foremost, through language. Now, it is the rule of breakdown, rather than accomplishment, that reigns. "Art often takes advantage of this property of desiring-machines by creating veritable group fantasies in which desiring-production is used to short-circuit social production, and to interfere with the reproductive function of technical machines by introducing an element of dysfunction."[22] This aesthetics is fully worked out in Deleuze's *Francis Bacon: Logique de la sensation.* Bacon's painting, with its aleatory techniques and extreme distortions of the human form, is taken as exemplary. Here, the human figure is grasped not as body or place, but rather as event.[23] The body, in Bacon, is presented as worked through by those invisible, spasmodic, libidinal forces that determine its existence: "Everything exists in relation to forces, everything is force. This constitutes deformation as an act of painting: it cannot be led either to a transformation of form or to a decomposition of elements."[24] This position values the realism of deformation over the idealism of transformation, and implicitely valorizes the relation between "eye and hand" over that of Merleau-Ponty's tandem of "eye and mind."[25] But even given Bacon's radical deformations of human physiognomy, there is a much more profound and disquieting metaphor at the core of Deleuze's model: the "body without organs."

The year 1972 marked the posthumous culmination of Artaud's role in a new aesthetics, with both the publication of *Anti-Oedipe* and with the Colloque de Cerisy on Artaud and Bataille organized by Philippe Sollers, whose journal *Tel Quel* presented Artaud's work since the early 1960s.[26] Yet only today can we gauge the full import of Artaud, taking advantage of the recent publication of the private notebooks of his last years, the *Cahiers de Rodez* and the *Cahiers du retour à Paris*.

Artaud's perpetual anxiety of loss already anticipates his fantasm of the "body without organs," a term that first appears in his radiophonic work, *Pour en finir avec le jugement de Dieu* (1947), and much later made famous in the anti-Oedipal theorization of Deleuze and Guattari:

> The body without organs is an egg: it is crisscrossed with axes and thresholds, with latitudes and longitudes and geodesic lines, traversed by *gradients* marking the transitions and the becomings, the destinations of the subject developing along these particular vectors. Nothing here is representative; rather, it is all life and lived experience.[27]

Artaud thematized an impossible, monstrous body, evoked in order to escape from the "limbo of a nightmare of bones and muscles," to circumvent and transcend what Bachelard spoke of as the "visceral imagination" or what Barthes termed "the grain of the voice." Citing the diatribe of *Pour en finir avec le jugement de Dieu*, this corporeal utopia of the "body without organs" is the ultimate mechanism of protection from God, man, and metaphysics:

> Man is sick because he is badly constructed.
> We must decide to strip him in order to scratch out this
>   animalcule which makes him itch to death,
>
>   god,
>   and with god,
>   his organs.
>
> For tie me down if you want to,
> but there is nothing more useless than an organ.
>
> When you have given him a body without organs,
> then you will have delivered him from all his automatisms
>   and restored him to his true liberty.[28]

Like the dreamwork, psychotic delirium is organized according to a corporeal symbolism, ultimately disclosing an unreachable, uninterpretable, originary nexus of significations which is none other than ineluctable realm of pure contingency. This nexus is precisely the point where the symbolic enters into history. Artaud's last works reveal, in all their terror, the chaotic depths of this nonessential, accidental circumstantiality. The body is the site of this contingency, where the magma of the imaginary and the exigencies of history manifest their connection in dreams, symbols, and acts.

Yet the symbolic may be contested on its own terms. Seemingly at the antipodes of Artaud's influence is the work of Marcel Duchamp. Artaud's passional, tragic struggle with interiority and his celebration of art as gesture must be contrasted with Duchamp's cool, ironic conceptualism. The Duchampian legacy is vast, manifested in such diverse aspects of modernism as antiretinalism, spectatorial participation, conceptualism, indeterminacy, celebration of the banal, chance determinations, systemics, aesthetic irony, ironic causality: in short, everything opposed to a corporeal, libidinal, gestural aesthetic. Broadly speaking, Duchamp's influence is evident in two distinct domains. First, the *aformal*, performative function of art is transformed by the readymade, which operates on the artist/spectator axis according to the principles that whatever the artist deems art constitutes the artwork, and that the spectator completes the artwork; thus, by definition, the artwork is never truly complete.[29] Second, the *formal* level of art is transformed by Duchamp's recognition that every aesthetic gesture and every performative act, even the most nihilistic, leaves a trace of virtual structures, matrices, plans, or situations. Thus the readymades, *chosen* but not created by the artist, provide a critique of art itself. Yet Duchamp also *constructed* many highly iconic, symbolic, and systemic works, exemplified by *La mariée mise à nu par ses célibataires, même.* Here, what is chosen is not the object, but the underlying systems or laws that structure the artwork. Duchamp established new relations between the nonretinal, cognitive, linguistic signified and the retinal signifiers.

Yet the importance of Duchamp in regard to any study of eroticism and contemporary aesthetics is made manifest on the level of the signifier: most of his works are in some manner imbued with the erotic. This is apparent beginning at least with his famous *Nude Descending a Staircase* (1911) and *La mariée* . . . (1915–23; also known as *The Large Glass*). It is so up through his little-known last works, such as the 1968 copperplate entitled *Morceaux choisis d'après Courbet*, which shows Courbet's *Woman with White Stockings* and a falcon and thus reveals, in Duchamp's pun, a *faux con* and a true one. It culminates in a sort of literal rendering of the earlier *Large Glass*, entitled *Étant Donnés: 1° La chute d'eau, 2° Le gaz d'éclairage*, where we see, through a peephole set in a wooden door, the exposed body of a nude woman in an outdoor setting.

One exhibition and catalogue, *Junggesellenmaschinen/Les machines célibataires*, organized by Harald Szeeman at the Kunsthalle in Berne in 1975, and passing through Paris at the Musée des Arts Décoratifs in 1976, established a decidedly erotic, indeed perverse, genealogy and teleology of Duchamp's iconography.[30] Based upon Michel Carrouges's notion of the "bachelor machine" as a delirious, solipsistic, onanistic mechanism, this exhibition surreptitiously and centrifugally expands the realm of Duchampianism beyond the art historical into the deepest regions of the psyche: erotic perversion, schizophrenic delirium, Art Brut, mediumistic expression, mysticism, alchemy, science fiction, sadomasochism, etc. Art history is, in a sense, circumvented by direct appeal to the phantasmatic origins of social and erotic production; Duchamp is seen as an avatar of a particularly modernist form of Eros.

In the theoretical realm, we find, in a very different context, the culmination of this approach in two distinct works. Within psychoanalytic theory, Guy Rosolato's aesthetics is based in great part on his analysis, "Étude des perversions sexuelles à partir du fétichisme," a study of fetishism as the prime contestation of the symbolic law.[31] Fetishism is the paradigmatic perversion, insofar as it replaces the Oedipal symbolic law with its own law and its own "cult" objects and libidinal ceremonies. For the fetishist, the intensity of pleasure is the sign that desire, and not the symbolic, is law. Parallel to his effort, Roland Barthes's *Fragments d'un discours amoureux* (1977) is a celebration of linguistic fetishization as a mode of singularity, as a *poesis particularis* of love. The maniacal, monological, heterological, perverse manifestations of love are expressed, and disparate fragments of behavior and appearance are recognized as revealing the truths of desire. Love, according to Barthes, demands a unique, intoxicating fetish, one which ultimately remains uncommunicable, and thus escapes all hermeneutics.

The uniqueness of a lover's discourse, like the singularity of an artwork, places it beyond all truth value. It is thus ultimately defenseless, without power or logic. This is precisely the reason why it is a conduit for joy. In this regard, need it be said that one must pass from the word to the act? Or must we insist that word is already act? In either case, I simply wish to repeat—in order to promote that passage toward joy—that art must be erotic and contentious, or it shall no longer be.

6   formations of subjectivity and sexual identity

I will open a studio where you go to have your picture "taken." You bring with you any photograph you like. After a small deposit, the photographer takes *the photograph from you, at which time the balance falls due.*

—Hollis Frampton

arcel Duchamp—the sign of a coherent system, and not the index of a man—signifies an ego both internally split and externally doubled, an ego that is the very *process* of instituting its own sign system while contesting the codes of everyday language from which that system is derived. In the notes for Duchamp's masterpiece, *The Large Glass—La mariée mise à nu par ses célibataires, même (The Bride Stripped Bare by Her Bachelors, Even)*—there is to be found a small diagram indicating the main iconographic axis of the *Glass's* arcane symbolic system. This diagram marks the difference between the top and bottom panels of the *Glass* as sexual difference itself:

MAR
———
CEL

This signifies, of course, the difference between the iconographic systems of the bride and her bachelors—"*mar*iée" and "*cél*ibataires"—a difference already inscribed in the syllables of Duchamp's name: *Mar/cel*.[1] The ambiguities, amphibologies, and duplicities that were to mark his life work are already apparent in his proper name.

Yet this ego, divided between male and female, was not only doubled by internal division, it was also redoubled by external projection. Monsieur Marcel Duchamp occasionally assumed the alter ego of Mademoiselle Rrose Sélavy—"Eros c'est la vie" (Eros is life). The linguistic rules of this division, this presumably "sexual" difference, are quite simply determined by phonetic coincidences: the declension of verbal structures and gender identification follows the system of signifiers, with complete disregard for the referential givens.[2] The Duchampian "subject construction" is apsychological, anti-essentialist, and arbitrary in relation to sexual difference. This difference is created by a play of signifiers within the textual system. The Duchampian *inscription* must not be confused with an existential *description*, since the form of the inscription, of the symbolic system, is ruled by a referential slippage resulting in ambiguity, and not by the desire for absolute epistemological rectitude. This is what Duchamp referred to as an "ironical causality," where each effect can be determined according to two or more causes, and where the structural *validity* of the "argument" or aesthetic form is in no way to be confused with the referential *truth* of that form.[3] As in any logical system, validity and truth remain on separate ontological levels and are only occasionally and coincidentally congruent.

Yet there *is* a representation, a photograph, of Rrose Sélavy: a 1921 Man Ray photograph of Duchamp in drag as Rrose Sélavy, whose hands are adjusting a fur collar. But these hands, as well as the hat "she" wears, are not those of Duchamp: they belong to Germaine Everling (Francis Picabia's mistress). As Duchamp claims in one of his epigrams, this is certainly "A charge de revanche; à verge de rechange" ("In exchange for a favor, a substitute penis").[4] As the persona of Duchamp is divided between masculine and feminine signifiers, so too is this apparently feminine alter ego split between feminine and masculine aspects. And it is not by chance that the head is of Duchamp and the hands are those of another: this difference is in accordance with Duchamp's aesthetic principles that entail the quest for a purely cognitive art, and a correlative denigration of retinal art, which is a function of craftsmanship. This valorization of the cognitive was codified by Duchamp in his theory of a "beauty of indifference,"[5] instantiated in his selection of "readymades." These ready-made objects, chosen by random selection, destroy all modes of aesthetic choice based upon classical notions of beauty and inaugurate a mode of aesthetic production closely allied with critical thought. Duchamp's insistence on the role of the spectator in the creative act may be considered in these terms, and may certainly play a role in the current debates on subject construction and spectatorial position: "All in all, the creative act is not performed by the artist alone; the spectator brings the work in contact with the external world by deciphering and interpreting its inner qualifications and thus adds his contribution to the creative act."[6]

The critical text thus becomes one of the signifieds of the artwork, and the spectator one of the protagonists of the narrative, by means of both identification and interpretation. And yet, this *aesthetic indifference* is paralleled by a *sexual indifference*: Duchamp's works are sexually overdetermined, dually (duplicitously) marked, and thoroughly mocking of the subject postion of precisely those spectators, those "critics," whose thoughts and reactions are to "complete" his work. We are, from the outset, one of the terms of his "ironic causality," and part of the ambiguity of his work stems from the very incongruities between Duchamp's wit and critical seriousness, between his duplicity and our desire for unambiguous complicity.

In this light, we might do well to remember what psychoanalytic theory teaches us about transsexualism: this psychological syndrome, this formation, is not determined by a quest for pleasure, but rather by a search for identity. It is narcissism and *not* a universal castration anxiety that oversees this project.[7] Hence this formation is organized according to the desired congruence between narcissism and sexual identity, between ego and ego ideal, where the ego ideal serves as the interface between the individual and societal collectivity. The libidinized ego of narcissism is manifested, externalized, in aesthetic sublimation, where personal phantasms are transformed into collectively available cultural objects. The art object is thus the sign of an inner psychological experience, of a phantasm, but this does not necessarily mean that it is a symptom, an effect: the art object is as much a sign of objective transformation as of subjective expression.

In both the instances of transvestism and the creation of artworks, internal structures of identity are projected into a public spectacle, hence made available for appropriation by the spectator, according to the phantasmic structure of the spectator's psyche. And it is precisely within the incongruence between the artist's and the spectators' phantasmatic formation that the ambiguities of the artwork lie. Similarly, it is in the terms of congruence between the two that the level of fascination with the artwork is to be discovered. The fascinating, uncanny, enigmatic aspect of the artwork is a function of the surprise in discovering in the external world a sign of our very desires, an expression of our most secret fantasies, a trace of our own psychological trajectories.

Primary narcissism is characterized by an absolute, almost divine desire for self-sufficiency. Thus it is not surprising that secondary narcissism—especially as manifested in the artwork—often reveals a search for immortality and the desire for the artist to be his or her own cause, *causa sui*. It is the desire to escape all artistic influence, i.e., to be totally *sui generis*.[8] Even so, secondary narcissism will, ironically, be oriented by the desire to identify with that parental persona that most lends itself to narcissistic libidinal cathexis.[9] This desire will be contested by a countercathexis serving as an ego-defense mechanism, in opposition to the threat to psychic security posed by the identificatory figure. Insofar as the artwork serves as the expression of such a defense mechanism, it is manifested as an *enigma* where the origin of the self in interpsychic relations is first lost and then recreated again within a solipsistic system of significations.

Insofar as aesthetic pleasure is partially a function of self-identity that determines spectatorial identification, the possibility of libidinal cathexis onto an artwork is a function of the coincidental congruence between the empirical mode of construction of the spectator's psyche and the ideal egological formations of narrative (or symbolic) subject construction in the artwork.

Duchamp's system is an extreme limit of this aesthetic will to break the signifying chain of identification, to create a system that is *sui generis* and apsychological. By means of the ambiguities of gender identification and subject position, his works foreground, on the very level of their materiality, these differences *as* the very meaning of the system. This precludes the possibility of univocal identification, which opens up the possibility of multiple, conflicting, sometimes ironic identificatory positions. The Duchampian system is art as metacritique: the inherent "meta-irony" engages the spectator precisely because no single spectatorial position may be determined as privileged, no single psychological identification valorized. It is a work for all and for none.

Returning to Marcel Duchamp/Rrose Sélavy, it should be noted that Duchamp's only attempt at the cinema—*Anémic cinéma* (1925–26)—is "signed" by Rrose Sélavy as its *"auteur."* The film's last shot is marked "Copyrighted by Rrose Sélavy 1926" and bears the fingerprint of Duchamp himself (and *not* that of Germaine Everling, whose hands are those of the photographed Rrose Sélavy). Thus Rrose *or* Marcel might be considered as the narrator of the nine declarative sentences that make up the text of this film, texts that are interspersed with optical spiral forms (thus intermingling the apparently incommensurable aesthetic domains of the cognitive and the retinal). Furthermore, there is textual evidence external to the film for this ambiguous authorial reference. One of the texts that appears in *Anémic cinéma*—"Esquivons les ecchymoses des Esquimaux aux mots exquis" ("Let us elude the ecchymosis of the Eskimos with exquisite words")—appeared earlier, in 1924, in the journal *391* as: "Rrose Sélavy et moi esquivons les ecchymoses des Esquimaux aux mots exquis" ("Rrose Sélavy and I elude the ecchymosis of the Eskimos with exquisite words"). Thus by means of the use of the pronominal shifter "moi" and the verbal declension in the first-person plural "esquivons" to relate Rrose and Marcel in the same act, the play of authorial difference is raised to yet another level. It is no longer Duchamp *as* Rrose Sélavy, but Duchamp *and* Rrose Sélavy, who are the narrative figures in this erotic filmic text.[10]

To suppress this dual relation and conflate the two figures into that of Rrose Sélavy as *auteur*—and then to divide it once again in terms of the difference between the referent of the nomination and the indexical referent of the fingerprint—is to problematize the very question of the artwork as simultaneously the expression of an identificatory pattern and the desire to break that structure and be one's own origin.

The title of another major work by Duchamp is *Tu m'* (1918), his last easel painting. This juxtaposition between the first-person singular and the second-personal singular pronominal shifters, presumedly addressed by the artist ("m' ") to the spectator ("tu") in a mode of rhetorical suspension, an ellipsis, indicates an unspecified action or state of affairs. The reflexivity of the "m' " indicates the action of the missing verb and object of the phrase. This relation, no doubt, is the very relation of the spectator to the artwork and artist, a relation that Duchamp specified as the very condition of the completion of the artwork. Yet the missing verb indicates that this relation is unspecifiable, polyvalent, and that the artwork is to remain perpetually incomplete, with the emptiness at its center being a function of both the artist's absence and the perpetual change of spectators. This series of variations is specified by the use of the pronominal shifter which, after all, can bear any enunciator as its subject or object.

Perhaps one aspect of the enigma of such works may be clarified by considering the lexical definitions of the archetypical pronominal shifter: "I." As *Webster's Dictionary* specifies:

> ²i/ . . . 1: the one who is speaking or writing . . . used as a nominative pronoun of the first person singular by one speaking or writing to refer to himself as the doer of the action . . . or the subject of a predicated condition . . . or sometimes in the predicate after forms of *be* . . . or in comparisons after *than* or *as* when the first term of the comparison is the subject of a verb . . . or in some absolute or elliptical constructions esp. when not used with a prepositional phrase or an adjective or a participle . . . or after *but* in a compound subject. . . . —see ME, MINE, MY; compare WE.

> [3]i/ . . . 1: someone possessing and aware of possessing a distinct and personal individuality: SELF, EGO.[11]

If Duchamp's work is grammatically structured by ambiguity, then it is logically ruled by paralogism.[12] While the term *paralogism* may indicate any form of logical fallacy, it is sometimes defined in the more specific sense of "a fallacy of arguing from the empty concept of the ego to its substantiality and eternality." Thus this sort of paralogism is a mode of the intrusion of narcissistic libido into logic. As such, this formal fallacy explains the shift of emphasis from the meaning of the first lexical entry of "I" (which is a linguistic definition) to the meaning of the second lexical entry for "I" (which is a metaphysical, indeed Cartesian, definition). This difference, this paralogism, might aid in understanding what is of the essence in Duchamp's artworks and in his critique of the artistic and spectatorial tradition, as well as what is at stake in the discussion of Hollis Frampton's work that follows.

Hollis Frampton met Marcel Duchamp. In a letter dated 16 July 1962, Frampton recounts the opening of a show of Yves Klein's work at Castelli's gallery in New York: "That was at a gathering where YK showed his movies = daubing very resilient, pubescent + naked ladies with scads of gold paint + having them roll around on canvas. Duchamp, asked what he thought, said: '. . . eh . . . ah . . . *ordure,* naturellement, mais . . . Klein, c'est ordure d'une sorte particulairement *française.*' (He approved of my *ad hoc* translation: JUST SOME MORE FRENCH SHIT. . . .)"[13] It might seem strange that Duchamp (whose texts in *Anémic cinéma* evince a violently erotic play of words) and Hollis Frampton (whose texts in *Poetic Justice* have a generically erotic narrative) should both be apparently appalled by Klein's film. Yet we might remember the major difference between these films: the erotic "narrative" or description in Duchamp's and Frampton's films is linguistic, and in both cases the protagonists are either not identifiable or ambiguously defined. On the other hand, the eroticism (or at least nudity) in Klein's film is rendered by the iconic character of the photographic process. In these different modes of presentation we find the divergence between the two lexical definitions of "I," as it is operative in the construction of the filmic text. Perhaps for Duchamp and Frampton a necessary precondition for developing a purely cognitive art was a metaphysical prudishness. Eroticism, suppressed on the iconic level, reappears on the linguistic level; the representational is transformed into an ambiguous indexicality.

It is clear that Frampton was influenced by Duchamp in both his aesthetics and his cinematic production, especially in *Poetic Justice* (1972), which like *Anémic cinéma* is one of the rare films composed almost entirely of a written text, where paratext serves as text.[14] Yet the major textual difference between these two films is that the texts in Duchamp's film are simple declarative sentences, without any apparent narrative connection, while the texts in Frampton's film are narratively structured. Yet both films do, in fact, determine narrative position by means of the linguistic shifter.

Poetic Justice is a film composed entirely of shots of a written filmscript. Beginning with an unnumbered shot of a pile of blank white pages on a table between a potted cactus and a coffee mug, successive shots reveal a filmscript of 240 shots—with one title or shot described per page—in four tableaux, ending with an unnumbered shot of a pile of blank white pages on which is placed a gray rubber glove. The text is divided into four parts, in a narrative of almost generic simplicity, where the protagonists are indicated solely by the use of the pronominal linguistic shifter, in either the indicative or possessive mood: (me, myself, you [second-person singular], you [second-person plural], yourself, your lover; my, your [second-person singular], your [second-person plural], your lover's). The *First Tableau* begins with a description of the scene (table, cactus, cup) itself, then proceeds to describe the protagonist placing three photographs of "your face" on a table, which "your hands" tear to pieces. "Your lover" enters the scene, and after "you" leave and disappear in the distance, "your lover" sorts the fragments of the photographs, which are complete but incorrectly sorted. The *Second Tableau* describes numerous scenes in which "you" and "your lover" figure, each scene immediately followed by "my hand" holding a photograph of that very same scene, culminating in a scene in which "you" and "your lover" embrace, naked, in a room. The *Third Tableau* describes "you" and "your lover" making love on a bed, while from outside the window of the room are described a multiplicity of diverse scenes of the world. The *Fourth Tableau* describes "you" and "your lover" in a room in which is found a stack of photographs on a table. As "you" film "your lover's" face, that face is hidden by an upraised photograph. Then "your lover's" hand holds up numerous photographs, depicting "yourself" and "your lover" in various poses and activities. In one sequence, the photographs are paired off, so that the first of each pair describes "yourself" in a scene, and the next describes "your lover" in the very same scene. The film ends with the following shots, where the narrator is reintroduced:

> #235. Your lover's hand is holding a still photograph of yourself, your lover and me enjoying a picnic on the grass.
> #236. Your lover's hand is holding a still photograph of myself, filming you and your lover.
> #237. Your lover's hand is holding a still photograph of my hand, writing this text.
> #238. Your lover's hand is holding a still photograph of myself, filming these pages.
> #239. Your lover's hand is holding a still photograph of my own face.
> #240. My hand covers a still photograph of my own face.
> And the final, unnumbered shot is of the pile of white pages on which lies a gray rubber glove.

The radicalness of both *Poetic Justice* and *Anémic cinéma*—two films that depict a linguistic paratext as the very image of the filmic text—has been analyzed in the literature.[15] As such, these films epitomize a supremely iconoclastic modernism, aiming at a purely conceptual art, where the filmic text attempts the ideal sublimation of the figural into the textual. But we are here concerned with a much narrower aspect of this filmed linguistic text, precisely the possibilities, complexities, and effects of presenting narrative where the pronominal shifter is not bound to a definite speaker. The implications of this usage may reveal both certain limitations in contemporary theories of spectatorial construction as well as the position of avant-garde cinema in relation to mainstream narrative cinema.

Emile Benveniste's "La nature des pronoms" (in *Problèmes de linguistique générale*) is one of the classic statements on the nature of deictics, the role of linguistic shifters.[16] There is no definite lexical meaning of any given pronominal shifter; its meaning is dependent upon the instance of speech in which it occurs, and not upon any lexical or syntactic structures. It thus operates according to an instrumental, pragmatic, existential usage or function. The shifter is not in a distinct class of reference, but rather refers directly to the act of discourse in which it is pronounced; it refers directly to the situated discourse of the present speaker. In such cases the subject-referent is *sui generis.*

The use of the pronominal shifter entails the very irruption of speech (*parole*) into language (*langue*), where language itself becomes possible because each locutor is posed as a subject—as an ego—and finds its place within the linguistic system. Thus the empty pronominal shifters as non- or auto-referential signs become full or bound by means of locution. It is precisely this shift from empty to full signs that permits Roman Jakobson (following Peirce) to claim that, "Shifters combine the two functions and thus belong to the class of symbols-indices."[17] (We might note that the shift from the empty, indexical, self-referential function to the full, symbolic, substantial function parallels the shift of lexical definitions of "I" discussed earlier. Not only is this difference, this shift, at the heart of Duchampian paralogisms and ambiguity, but—as contemporary psycholinguistics, structural anthropology, and deconstructive philosophy have shown—it is also the source of the major category error at the core of Western metaphysics.)

The fundamental polarity in language is structured according to the difference between the shifters "I" and "you," upon which the pragmatic functions of communication are founded.[18] While this relationship is reversible within discourse, the terms of the relationship are neither equal nor symmetric. The "I," the ego, is always in a position of transcendence to the "you." Furthermore, this dissymmetry is related to a different mode of deictic dissymmetry: that of the difference between the poles *I/you* and *he/she/it*. While the former are autoreferential within the moment of discourse, the latter third-person terms are a sort of abbreviation for the inclusion of the objective world into the deictic field. This third-person referent is always independent of the present moment of discourse, that very moment that determines the referent "I" or "you."

As the empty shifter becomes full by means of the specificity of locution, it also becomes sexually marked. The difference between the spoken and the written use of the pronominal shifter is thus of prime importance. The spoken shifter is necessarily sexually marked by the gender of the speaker (except, of course, in passages of quotation, the use of metalanguage, and other such deviations from the self-referential pronominal usage in everyday speech). The written shifter *may* be sexually marked within the narrative context, but may also (as in the case of the textual system of *Poetic Justice*) remain sexually ambivalent. (Note that this is the case for the first- and second-person singular pronominal shifters: the third-person singular shifter is already sexually marked. Yet even such apparent marking may, by the very rhetorical structure of the text and in certain idiomatic usages, be either ambiguous or even the opposite of the stated term. For example, the synecdochic use of "he" for the male *and* female subject dissimulates, rather than reveals, sexual differences within the text; in the plural, there is the archaic case of the royal "we.")

The radicalness of the text of *Poetic Justice* is due precisely to the unbound nature of its deictic terms, entailing a sexually unmarked subject construction, used as a device of spectatorial distanciation. In most narrative films—even of the Brechtian sort—the binding of the deictic structure to a visually represented character entails the possibility of spectatorial identification, be it through libidinal cathexis or countercathexis. The linguistic modes of spectatorial insinuation into the filmic narrative depend upon the specific relationships between: (1) the narrative and characterological construction of the film along with the ideal spectator that is consequently implied by this structure; *and* (2) the empirical psychological constitution of the spectator, which determines the specific mode of identification, either in accordance with or in deviation from that ideal construction of the spectatorial subject.

The susceptibility of identification—in both its positive and negative modes—depends upon the degree of adequation between the subject construction in the film's narrative/ rhetorical system and the phantasmatic construction of the spectatorial subject. These indentificatory relations may be schematized as follows: (1) identification (assimilation; narcissistic love); (2) attraction (appropriation; anaclitic love); (3) rejection (repulsion; hatred or rivalry); and (4) indifference (foreclosure; denial of the paradigm of love relations).

In turn, each of these syndromes, each of these modes of desire, of identification, may be cathected upon a different cinematic structure: (1) a character in the film; (2) the narrator (who may be a character in the film); or (3) the camera (which is the implied position of an unseen spectator, and may be either a character, the narrator, or omniscient).

There is clearly no definitive, pregiven correlation between spectatorial gender and identificatory patterns in any given film. While each film will posit an ideal spectator and normative psychic mode of relation to that ideal, this does not preclude the possibility of identifications that operate against the dictates of this ideal—and in terms of mainstream cinema one might almost insist, ideological—system of subject construction. This discrepancy implicitly contests the axiomatic system that structures the film's narrative. The axiomatics of mainstream cinema posits a rectitude between such subject construction and spectatorial identification, in terms of a normatively structured relationship. While the psychological paradigms of filmic subject construction remain necessarily fixed by the narrative system, the paradigms of spectatorial subject construction—including the vast range of possibilities such as neurosis, psychosis, autism, fetishism, perversion, sadomasochism, transvestism, homosexuality, bisexuality, and of course, heterosexuality, etc.—differ from spectator to spectator. Hence varied and even multiple spectatorial identifications are always possible.

If the quest for identity (sexual and otherwise) is a function of the cathexis of narcissistic libido, then this very same narcissism constitutes the predications of the locutory "I."[19] As the pronominal shifter entails the eruption of subjectivity (and consequently of libido) into language, it serves as the very articulation of the linguistic field, an articulation that organizes that field as the place of contradiction, of dialectics, between "you" and "I," between self and other. As Benveniste explains regarding the relationship between "you" and "I": "It is within a dialectical reality englobing the two terms and defining them by their mutual relation that we discover the linguistic foundation of subjectivity."[20] The ego is constituted within language as a diacritical, dialectical field, articulated within a cultural/historical situation literally vis-à-vis other subjects, other egos. And it is precisely the structure of this linguistic field that guarantees the presumed homogeneity of the subject as a transcendental ego.

The ontological implications of these structural differences serving as models of subjectivity may be clarified by considering two basic paradigms of contemporary philosophy and their influence on the contemporary debate on subject construction. These paradigms are the dialectical and the phenomenological systems of epistemology, represented in their major instances by Hegel and Emmanuel Levinas. For Hegel, language is fundamentally an alienating structure: the logical structure of language—universal reason—rules the transformation of particularity into generality. Reason excludes the singular. Everything expressed in language is necessarily universalized; the specificity of my speech is subverted by the historical process—the dialectic—which takes up my words and deeds and transforms them into something wholly other, something alienated. (*Parole* is always betrayed by *langue*.) This system of transformation determines the very constitution of the ego, so that the subject is always, following Julia Kristeva's terminology, a "subject in process." The "I" as a universal figure can only attain self-consciousness by recognizing the universality of its particular condition. This objectification may only be achieved through recognition by the other, through a struggle with the other, within the dialectical (dialogic) relationship between master and slave. Hence this mode of interpersonal relationship is foundationally asymmetrical, a condition, as we have seen, fully structured into the linguistic system by means of the different modes of pronominal shifters.

In his analysis of Hegel's influence on Lacan, Anthony Wilden suggests that while there is a subject function in language due to the substitutability of shifters, there is no such possibility on the gestural level, nor can the gesture be taken up as a metastatement.[21] The gesture thus bears an absolute subjective value. It is perhaps in the thought of Emmanuel Levinas that subjective particularity receives its major ontological statement, revealed in terms of a subject whose particularity is revealed in the very epiphany of the face as a pure, direct, ethical imperative that is irreducible to any systematic thought, to any language system. In his magnum opus, *Totality and Infinity*, Levinas shows how it is not only the gesture, but the individual characteristics of the face itself—as the paradigm of all gestural possibility—that bears the trace of the absolute subject, of the Other, as an infinite immanence both asymmetric to and transcendent to myself.[22] The face is an epiphany where what is literally vis-à-vis operates as the determinative factor of subjectivity within the cultural/historical field. In other words, the linguistic shifters are bound, filled, fully predicated within the speech act. This filling of the shifter is, in a sense, the function of an icon: the face as the very locus of speech. The face is the icon of the self. Unlike the Hegelian dialectic, this relationship indicates a relationship of transcendence, not of power or domination. Thus the speech, discourse, that proceeds from such an absolute alterity guarantees that "language accomplishes a relation between terms that break up the unity of a genus."[23] The genus of "man," "humanity," or "subjectivity" is subverted by recognition of the infinite transcendence of the Other, signified by the trace, the face. Yet in this sense, "to signify is not equivalent to presenting oneself as a sign, but to expressing oneself, that is, presenting oneself in person."[24] Subjectivity, intersubjectivity, is founded upon *person*-alization, and here the relationship between signifier and signified is not founded upon correlation or rectitude, but rather upon an absolute, nonrepresentable difference. This results, according to Levinas, in the very "unsettling of intentionality" (in contradistinction to the apparent rigidity of the noesis/noema relationship in classic Husserlian phenomenology.)[25]

The difference between the Hegelian and the Levinasian paradigms respectively is the difference between: the locus of subjectivity in a codified linguistic system (*langue*) and the locus of subjectivity in the speech act (*parole*); the self as self-concept and the self as presence; the self as process of universalization through negation and the self as concrete particularization through an ethical imperative. For Hegel, the self is a function of the work of negativity where the "I" is always caught up in a movement of alienation, objectification, and universalization; for Levinas, the self is never divorced from the exigencies of the flesh.

These paradigms, which we have seen to be already inscribed in the Duchampian alter ego, may also be seen to be central to the current feminist debates on subject construction and spectatorial identification in the cinematic apparatus, especially as concerns the problem of sexual difference.[26] Schematically outlined, the opposing limit models are: an essentialist model, whereby sexual differentiation is a function of physical sexual difference; and an antiessentialist model, whereby sexual differentiation is a function of identificatory positioning within discourse. This subject construction is posed in relation to either corporeal or linguistic paradigms, a difference noted above within the aporia of a linguistic "I" and a physical/metaphysical "I"—an aporia central to the Duchampian paralogism that is expressed by the difference between linguistic and iconic representation in *Anémic cinéma*—that marks the difference between Hegel and Levinas.

In the current debate, the essentialist model is exemplified by the work of Luce Irigaray.[27] The subject, according to Irigaray, is constituted within an Oedipal "circuit of exchange." The subject, the "I," is sexually marked within the discursive field according to specular identification. Thus the body itself, bearer of sexual difference, simultaneously becomes the common *object* of exchange and the *subject* of enunciation. Yet the very limits of such placement within the signifying system are determined by the subject's corporeal constitution. Quite simply, there are different paradigms of masculine and feminine sexuality, which in turn mark the differences of subjective (deictic) enunciation. The insertion of the object within discourse is already gender marked; knowledge is a function of the meaningful embodiment of the world. Thus the body is supremely meaningful. Yet since the subject is not pure denotation but a series of connotations, it does have a future, it is a critical, open system.

The antiessentialist model is exemplified by certain works of Kristeva. According to Kristeva, the subject is fundamentally a "subject in process" or a "subject on trial."[28] The pronominal shifter is the hinge of the signifying process, which determines a nonlocalizable subjectivity. Thus the unity of the ego, a transcendental ego insofar as it is unified, is that of the coherence of the sign and predicate synthesis, a coherence effected by the speaking subject within a given linguistic system. Yet since the relation between the signified and the referent is one of displacement and not of identity, this synthesis is marked by a radical internal rupture, a sort of uncertainty principle. The subject can either accept or reject the Oedipal law; due to the equivocal possibilities of deictic structure within enunciation, the subject is the place of contradiction. Hence the manner in which the dialectical process is inscribed in language. This permits an "incessant permutation of shifters," a sort of confusion of tongues and identities. In itself, the body is non-sense. To attack the unity of the sign and syntax (as was the quest of early modernism) is to attack, dis rupt, the unity of the subject. This is precisely, according to Kristeva, the role of the avant garde. And it is in this light that we might investigate the extent to which Frampton's film *Poetic Justice* offers immediate, if disquieting, access to this problematic.

In "Frampton's Sieve," Annette Michelson signals the importance of the pronominal shifter in *Poetic Justice* in terms of the dislocation, confusion of coordinates, and the defeat of diegetic construction it entails. One level of this dislocation is effected such that, "With the final shot, in which an empty glove is cast upon the script, the collapse of the narrative's authorial 'I' into that of the maker of the first-order film is effected, and the full range of the *mise-en-abîme* is disclosed."[29] This glove serves as an indeterminate index of the script-writer/*auteur* of the film and the filmscript. Similarly, the fingerprint in the final title of *Anémic cinéma* serves as an index of *auteur*—Marcel Duchamp—and possibly, but not necessarily, of Rrose Sélavy, who is the putative *author*/narrator, but whose *hands* are not those of the actual *craftsman*, the fingerprinted Duchamp. Thus the relation between *auteur* and narrator remains ambiguous, indeterminate. This dislocation in *Poetic Justice* is further complicated by the very role of the shifter in the filmic text, as regards spectatorial identification. As the empty form of the pronominal shifter permits contradictory spectatorial identifications—such that the shifter cannot be unequivocally filled or bound—there is no iconic origin of enunciation, and thus no definitive term of identificatory possibility. (The reason for this, of course, is because in this film, the shifter is presented solely in a written mode and is never spoken, thus the "discrete and singular act" of its discursive instance is never "actualized in utterance by a speaker":[30] what remains is the equivocation of universalized possibility.) In this text the shifters maintain their linguistic purity without being tainted by an existential referent.

Not only does the shifter remain empty here, but there is not even a clue as to how spectatorial identification may be distributed between the different narrative positions of the respective characters. Where the shifter is bound (as in all

Hollywood narrative mainstream cinema), enunciation distributes the interlocutory roles among the speakers. These roles are reinforced by the play of gazes (even, and especially, that of the camera gaze) as it entails the reversibility of subject and object, and orders the gender marked identificatory patterns. But with the unbound shifters of *Poetic Justice*, the distribution of the interlocutory roles within the sparse, generic narrative is of open-ended referentiality, and thus ambiguous. Thus the narrative structure of the film is detotalizing, without any psychological denotation. Since the characters may be male *or* female, in heterosexual *or* homosexual relations, all contingent modes of spectatorial identification are possible. Thus the very problematic of identification itself is foregrounded by being disrupted.

Most probably, the statistically dominant mode of identification is with the "you" of the text, which seems to be addressed to the spectator. But even this mode of identification is dependent upon just one possible imaginative mode of identification, one type of eidetic variation, which is by no means universally operative. What must be considered is the difference between "embodied" and "disembodied" imagination.[31] These descriptive modes of imaginative events or spectatorial identification determine subject position: the self is described either from its own corporeal position (embodied) or else from a subject position outside itself (disembodied). Thus depending upon whether the imaginative identificatory field is organized according to an embodied or a disembodied relation to one's own enunciatory position, the identification with the characters in *Poetic Justice* would respectively be with the "you" or with the "I" (narrator) of the text. The problem of sexual differentiation in this text is highlighted by being eliminated: there is only sexual indifferentiation. Desire is neither appropriated nor suppressed, and the fetishization of the gaze is left literally without its proper libidinal, partial object. We have the presentation of what, most disquietingly, may be termed the "putative subject," a subject always constructed according to our own narcissism, yet always lacking the source of the gaze by which that narcissism is ordained.

But what then is the "real" subject of this film? What is Frampton's own relation to the narrative, to the pronominal positions of the text? Does he partake of the first-order or the second-order narrative? Does he fill in the shifter "I," or is rather the authorial glove that he fills?

The ego exists by means of its mechanisms of defense: defenses against the instincts, the superego, the world, and others. As Anna Freud explains in *The Ego and the Mechanisms of Defense*, one means of defense is the neurotic denial of anxiety-producing reality by means of fantasy. Yet what is claimed for neurosis as a defense mechanism may, *mutatis mutandis*, obtain for both the psychotic and the artist: "In order to avoid suffering, it checks the development of anxiety and inflicts deformities upon itself."[32] Such deformities are manifested as both the latent content of the artwork-as-symptom and as the formal aspect of the artwork's manifest structure. Yet the difference between the mechanisms of neurosis and the artwork must be seen within the broader problematic of sublimation, i.e., within nonrepressive cathexes and transformations of libidinal energy. Sublimation is not mere reaction formation. Thus perhaps the model of reactive *and* active libido would be most appropriate for the differentiation between neurotic and sublimatory modes of ego development. This would respectively determine the difference between neurotic reaction formation as a substitute pleasure, a defense, aimed at the diminution of anxiety (thus a transformation of desire) and sublimated repetition as the very continuation of desire.[33] Thus the very same forms, expressed as neurotic symptom or artistic fantasy, would either be a function of repression or sublimation. Only in the analytic situation can this difference be determined, within the general context of the specific life forms that structure the authorial situation. Nevertheless, the structural relationships between psychopathological and sublimated expression may certainly be revelatory in any given hermeneutic of the artistic text.

Throughout *The Anxiety of Influence* and *Agon*, Harold Bloom, following the Lacanian assimilation of psychic operations to linguistic forms, shows how the ego defenses are modeled on rhetorical forms, how "the defenses are tropes."[34] The particular tropic structure of poetic language serves as a defense against the "anxiety of influence." This is the manifestation of the desire to be the absolute, uninfluenced origin of one's own works, of one's own self: it is a quest for priority. The poetic will is ego defense: "Poetry is the anxiety of influence, is misprision, is a disciplined perverseness. Poetry is misunderstanding, misinterpretation, misalliance."[35] Hollis Frampton too understood poetic influence in almost precisely these same terms: "The mode we call reading entails a correct extrapolation of the axiomatic substructure from the artist's immediately apprehensible tradition. Once the set of axioms has been isolated and disintricated, the artists may proceed to modify it in any of four ways: by substitution, constriction, augmentation, or by displacement."[36] We might note that these four types of modification not only present a typography of rhetorical types similar to those of classical rhetoric, but that they are also assimilable to the Freudian hermeneutic presented in *The Interpretation of Dreams*, which reveals the modes of the dreamwork in terms of condensation (substitution), displacement, conditions of representability (a type of constrictive system of rules), and secondary elaboration (augmentation). This broad similarity certainly bears upon the immediate relations between primary process libidinal figuration and secondary process sublimatory aesthetic production. To continue the parallel between Bloom's and Frampton's hermeneutic, we should review the latter's following considerations:

> All axiomatic sets that derive in any of these four ways from the mode we have called "reading" have one thing in common: they entirely supersede their predecessors, and thus, sooner or later, assume the historical role of all norms. In the moment that a new axiom vanishes into the substrate of an art, it becomes vulnerable. On the other hand, this is not true of those novel structural assumptions that derive from the mode that we have called "misreading." The incorrectly read or imperfectly disentangled compositional assumption invariably remains to haunt the intellectual space usurped by its successor.[37]

Art is a mode of fantasy structured by the desire to escape the anxiety of influence. While denial in pure fantasy can exist only so long as it is not contradicted by reality testing, denial in words and deeds—which includes aesthetic production as a type of "deed"—is similarly internally conditioned by the exigencies of reality testing, as well as being externally conditioned: "dramatization of fantasies in word and act requires a stage in the outside world."[38] It is precisely these conditions of dramatization, these conditions of representability, that we must consider in the present analysis. If art is a mode of phantasmatic production, then criticism is a mode of reality testing. Yet if, as Duchamp insists, the spectator, which includes the critic as a special case, completes the artwork, then somehow the critic's desire, the theoretician's desire, to rewrite the work by writing *about* the work reveals the very desire to be influenced, to appropriate the work of the other as one's own. Thus the ironic, identificatory relationship between artist and spectator revolves around the artwork as the place of representation, as the very condition of representability of one's own anxiety *of* and *for* influence. But not only does representation play a role in this procedure: the very avoidance of representation—iconoclasm—is always at the horizon of this ego defensive activity.

In *Poetic Justice,* the linguistic pronominal shifters which determine the protagonist's relations and the spectatorial identification *and* the photographs (invisible to us) of the protagonists that are displayed and "taken" are equally ambiguous and polyreferential:

> —My hand places a black-and-white photograph of your
>   face on a table.
> —Your hands lift a stack of photographs.
> —Your lover's hand is holding a still photograph of yourself, sipping wine.
> —My hand covers a still photograph of my own face.

We must ask, within the larger context of Frampton's work and the art historical influences on his work, what is the meaning of these invisible photographs? What remains to "haunt the intellectual space" whose influence Frampton himself usurped?

The major influence on Frampton's photographic work was Edward Weston. As Christopher Phillips claims in his analysis of Frampton's photography: "Looking back from the end of the 70's, Frampton recognized Weston's constrictive Law of the Father as an instance in which 'the mysteries are offered, but the rites of passage are withheld.' "[39] We must investigate Frampton's own understanding of these mysteries, in order to consider how his work may serve as our own hermeneutic rite of passage.

Writing of photography, Weston's claim that "the artist must be able to visualize his final result in advance" is understood by Frampton as being not merely the sign of pragmatic proficiency, of technical mastery, on Weston's part. It is, more markedly, a trope for the very style of Weston's work, a trope that, we shall see, recurs in Frampton's own work as the *literal* rendition, the literal mode, of *Poetic Justice*.

Frampton reads the history of photography in terms of one of the central ontological features of the photographic enterprise: the lack of a temporal dimension. "Much of the early history of still photography may be looked upon as the struggle of the art to purge itself of temporality."[40] And it is in Weston's work that he finds the culmination of this tradition, the ultimate photographic expression of this desire: "Weston is everywhere concerned, as are so many other still photographers, with the annihilation of time."[41] In terms of Bloom's reading of the anxiety of influence, this elimination of temporality is a manifestation of the revenge of a strong poetic will: "The poetic will is an argument against time."[42] Poetic substitution—substitution by tropes—is the transformation of the "it was" into an "it is," and the subsequent transformation of this "it is" into an "I am." Thus following Nietzsche's analysis of *ressentiment*, Bloom sees the strong poetic will as being the willful transformation of past contingencies into the very form of one's present existence. The self is reconstituted as the absolute source of priority by means of the dissimulation of alterity as origin.

This voiding of the photograph of temporal reference is apparent in Weston's style. In Frampton's analysis, "Weston, more and more often, simply centered his figure, outside time and within the nominal spatial ground of the photographic artifact."[43] This results in an abstraction leading to decontextualization, typification, and to the rendering of objects as anonymous and "faceless."[44] It results in a "generic space."[45] As we have seen, this is also precisely the result of the use of the pronominal shifter in *Poetic Justice*, where we find a generic narrative and an ambiguous, faceless subject, whose very anonymity ironically implicates the spectator within the narrative.

The "poetic justice" of this film—"poetic justice" being a figure of speech for irony—is that Frampton reverts to the prephotographic (profilmic) moment of previsualization in finding the images for this film: paratext is presented as text, script as image. By a temporal shift to the "origins" of the artwork in a pre-text, Frampton ironically attempts to overcome the influence of origins in an ironic reversal of means and ends. The invisibility of the photographic "images" mentioned in the text, the lack of iconic images in the film, and the very making of films, a temporal art, all serve as Frampton's ultimate reversal of Weston's influence. The full iconic signs of the master are parodied by empty signs, absent icons. While Weston's photographs, according to Frampton, *"aspire* to the monumental permanence of empty signs,"[46] Frampton's film, *Poetic Justice, achieves* the permanence of empty signs. Weston's work is thus cognitively consumed in and reaches its logical conclusion in Frampton's film just as in general photography is subsumed by cinema: "A still photograph is simply an isolated frame taken out of the infinite cinema."[47] Weston's influence was overcome both by an ironic reversal that transformed his works into empty signs *and* by being appropriated within another medium.

Yet despite the abstraction, the generic nature of both Weston's photographs and Frampton's film, they both partake of an apparent eroticism. Frampton notes that "Weston is invincibly propelled toward the sexualization, the genitalization even, of everything in sight."[48] But since, according to

Frampton, eroticism is a particular mode of knowing—arguing, in fact, that "nothing, including ourselves, can fully be known until it is somehow made the object of desire"[49]—this corporeal mode of knowledge depends upon the physical and temporal body of the object of desire. Deprived of this temporal, gestural, lived body, the desired object becomes a "brief, experimental fetish." As temporality is abolished in the still photograph—and abolished a fortiori in Weston's photography—a defective mode of knowledge is established. This defect is that of the fetish object. The fetish is the sign of the refusal of sexual differentiation in a partial object, as well as the refusal of that ontogenetic temporality whereby such differentiation is established. It entails the denial of recognizing any sexual form other than that of the self.

Only the cinema can rectify this defective mode of knowledge by reversing the abolition of temporality in the photographic icon, and by eliminating the fetishized object. Thus the partial, fetishized objects of Weston's abstraction are lost within Frampton's presentation of erotic scenes in an iconoclastic mode. Frampton maintained the erotic content of narration—the very basis of sublimatory activity and of poetic will—while refusing Weston's iconic fetishization. He replaced the iconophilia of a full world with the iconoclasm of an empty self; he voided the "I" of any possible reference to Weston's influence, indeed to any influence whatsoever, in order to claim his own voice. Hence the double irony, perhaps a Duchampian "meta-irony," that rules this filmic narrative. By eliminating one ironic structure (fetishization as the substitution of a symbolic phallus for the lack of a real penis), a higher level of irony is established, where there is a reversibility, in the film's characterological reference, between self and other.

By means of this process of emptying the self-referential pronominal shifters of all reference, the spectator is forced to undergo a defetishization in relation to the filmic text, is forced to realize the structures of both sexual and personal (identificatory) difference. In *Poetic Justice* the erasure of the subject is guaranteed by an aberrant use of deictics that defines a universality of subjective reference. The lack of a univocal mode of spectatorial identification is a function of this universalization: the text is ultimately meaningless precisely because it is universally meaningful. Asexual universal rationality, while an adequate defense against past fetishization, is an inadequate expression of the constitution of the self at risk in that very fetishization.

According to Bloom, the poetic figuration that is the will's defense against time is Eros itself, Eros as the underlying force behind the transformational processes of sublimation. In *Poetic Justice* there is a self-conscious repetition of desire manifested by a hyperbolic irony, i.e., within a system fully void of erotic iconography, where even the very form of the self is ambivalent. This "erasure of form," this threat to the visibility of desire, turns the paratext-as-text of the film into a metatext, a critique of classical Hollywood cinema's mode of fetishization and identification. Spectatorial fascination is shattered precisely because ego identification is thrown completely back upon the spectator, where in most cases this identificatory imperative is ignored. Hence the film is deemed boring. But no more boring than the self that makes this claim. The fascination of this film is not in what it shows of the desire of others, but rather in what it conceals from others and reveals to ourselves: our own desires.

"There is no camera in the room."

7   acting, identity, and scenarization

*I was lying beside a nude woman and was asked to look at her legs. I
stared at them for some time, but couldn't quite find the proper way
to respond. It seemed to me to be a problem of logic. I finally realized
that I would never discover the exact response since I was really not
very good in mathematics.*

—Account of a patient to Joyce McDougall
"Scène primitive et scénario pervers"

Freud begins his case history, "A Case of Paranoia Running
Counter to the Psychoanalytical Theory of the Disease"
(1915), with a methodological proviso: "I will say that I have
altered the milieu of this case in order to preserve the incognito of those concerned, but that I have altered nothing else. I
consider it an undesirable practice, however excellent the mo-
tive may be, to alter any detail in the presentation of a case."[1]
This alteration of milieu is, in fact, a necessary precondition
of all scenarization and theorization. An investigation of its effects on every level of discourse will aid in establishing a
hermeneutic procedure whereby the relations between analyst
and analysand, interpretor and personage, may be revealed in
their complexity and complicity. Yet, as a constant methodological proviso, we must remember that no representation or
model can duplicate or explain all aspects of the thing represented or analyzed, and we must beware of the difficulties of
analogical reasoning, which often leads to the confusion of
things with the very forms derived from them.

The impulse to theorize might be understood as the
ultimate limit of identificatory depersonalization. Theorization maintains an existential derealization/depersonalization
where the presumed universalization of identification—the

identification with *all* others—effects a final loss of self in an abstract moment. This moment may be deemed rationalized self-consciousness (the finalization of the Hegelian dialectic), but it is actually a flight from the self and its idiosyncrasies (the motivation of Marxist notions of alienation), a movement toward authorial incognito. Theorization thus entails an extreme instance of the splitting of the ego. Consider again Freud's disclaimer cited above: it is precisely according to what we may term the "syndrome of theorization" that Freud's alternation of milieu—the "suppression of characteristic details"—may be understood. The epistemophilic impulse to theorize necessitates the move from particular to universal; Freud's presumed concern to guard his patients' anonymity, the concern to avoid potential embarrassment, is but a narrative device which dissimulates the ruses of his rationalizing theoretical position. Rationalization within the Freudian scenario is a reduction of explanation to the narrative of the Oedipal scene, a scenarization that serves as the master narrative of metapsychology. The theorizing impulse is a fortiori an iconoclastic impulse—as is already attested to by Plato at the very origins of Western metaphysical systematization and the theorization of poetics.[2] Perhaps a more contemporary iconoclasm might guide our own investigations of the iconophilic relations between metapsychology and film theory.

In Freud's analysis of the case of paranoia cited above— where the complexities of the primal scene are revealed and examined—the following aspects of the analytic scenario and narrative are of special interest for our project: (1) on the level of the female patient's narrative: (a) the play of substitutions and transpositions entailed by the paranoid mechanism vis-à-vis the primal scene; (b) the multifarious modes of identification and the valences of cathexis in the scenario; (2) on the level of Freud's narrative: (a) the alteration of milieu (and the consequent suppression of detail and nomination) in recounting the scene; (b) the manner in which this alteration parallels and doubles the relation between the primal scene and the paranoid scene, a doubling established as a theoretical conceit permitting the universalization of a particular model of scenarization.

This analysis purports to reveal the origins of scenarization itself according to the unconscious conditions of representability through the ego-defense mechanism of the splitting of the ego conceived as re/mis/identification. Hence the necessity of revising the scenario. To analyze the change of milieu—which may ultimately result in a change of identification, a change of personality—will reveal the origins of narrative and the limits of iconography.

In Freudian metapsychology, the primal scene (primal phantasm) serves as an existential a priori of identificatory activity.[3] It simultaneously reveals the origins of sexuality in a scenario of sexual aggression *and* the origins of the self through the narcissistic wound entailed by such primal spectatorship. The primal scene is the most general and concentrated phantasmatic structure, manifesting the diverse possibilities of the Oedipal complex, the variations of which it generates.[4] The primal scene thus entails the channeling of desire according to the relational scheme which it imposes: the phantasm does not reveal the object of desire, but represents the very scene of desire.[5] This scenarization of desire is a fortiori a function of the primal scene, the phantasm of phantasms. The primal scene is always already present as phantasm, not as reality, and is thus already determined by the symbolic order of the unconscious, with *its* own conditions of representability. "The origin of phantasms is integrated into the very structure of the primal phantasm."[6] The primal scene furnishes the conditions of the possibility of psychic existence; nevertheless, the outcome and eventual resolution of the Oedipal complex which follows is all the while dependent upon the real, contingent factors of the particular experience which gave rise to the original phantasm.

The fact that phantasms are so varied is accounted for by the polyvalent aspect of the primal scene. The libidinal/phantasmatic linkage of the primal scene's three figures occurs as follows: the figures seen (father and mother) are linked in an active/passive activity; the third figure (child-spectator) is in turn linked to the other two as a passive figure in relation to the active couple. The Oedipal complex scenarized in the primal phantasm can either structure (as ego-defense mechanism) or destructure (as an ego-splitting device) consciousness in the process of personality formation. This occurs according to the contingent particularities of identifications, fixations, associations, etc. Thus the unconscious field—where there is a continual decomposition and recomposition, a continual recombination, of elements—is at the origin of all narrative.[7] Narrative structure is determined by the very changes, the differences, between possible and actual scenarizations. Such narrative is founded according to the combination of unconscious elements, with the possibility that any one of these elements (and even all of them simultaneously) may represent the self, as Freud revealed in *The Interpretation of Dreams*, and as poets and writers have long known. The primal phantasm is the explication of the origin of the self vis-à-vis the other, where the self is differentiated from the other in terms of the organization of the scenario; and where the other is always an identificatory possibility for the self, an ultimate, ideal transformation of the ego. Thus, in a play of Oedipal permutations, the goal is the delimitation of a place sometimes empty, sometimes full, for the subject.[8] (As we shall see, when the subject occupies more than one place in this permutational scheme, the result is often a pathological condition.) In order to reveal the hermeneutic value of this scenarization, we must investigate the permutational and identificatory possibilities of this Oedipal mechanism, whereby the subject's psychic existence is organized through the symbolic scenarization of the anterior structure of the primal scene.

The organization of personality/persona is a function of ego-defense mechanisms. These defense mechanisms—turning against the self, denial, reversal into the opposite, projection, etc.—have been homologized (in Lacanian metapsychology) with basic rhetorical structures. In turn, these tropes and figures may serve as the critical articulation of the relation between subjectivity and the artwork, in a structural and perhaps allegorical (but not causal) mode. Freud sketches out the possible permutations of the basic type of cathexis, the love/

hate relationship, between subject positions designated as "I," "she," and "he," schematized in the following transformations of the basic, archetypal relation, "I love him":[9]

Contradiction
I don't love him. (persecution)
I love her. (erotomania)
She loves me. (erotomania)
He loves her.
He doesn't love me. (persecution)

Non-Contradiction
I don't love her. (sadomasochistic relation to the mother, hiding paranoia and homosexuality.)
She doesn't love me. (ditto)
She doesn't love him. (perverse relationship, manifesting the separation of the parents.)
He doesn't love her. (ditto)

Other Forms
I love only myself. (megalomania)
I love nobody. (megalomania)

This analytic combinatory system charts out the possible personal relations—intersubjective positions—derived from the relata of the Oedipal scene: persecution, erotomania, jealousy, megalomania, homosexuality, heterosexuality, etc.

We may propose that this combinatory system be utilized as a hermeneutic model revealing the paradigmatic modes of spectatorial identification and subject positioning within aesthetic narrative structures, especially in regard to film studies. Each position in this system defines a different mode of subjectivity, a different psychological syndrome—any one syndrome being not necessarily exclusive of the others—thus constituting different means of living through the diverse effects of the primal scene, different types of relationships with others, and different modes of symbolization. Patterns of identification between spectator and personage must be defined according to these psychological complexities: there is no spectator *simpliciter*, male or female. Identification is always partial, fragmented, mixed; total identification would be delirium. Ultimately, a "logic of the particular" (one most certainly not blind to sexual difference, nor to different psychological syndromes) must be adapted in film criticism, all the while taking into account the descriptive attractions and epistemological difficulties of psychologism and biographism. The self must not be reduced to a type; yet the exigencies of stereotypicality and mass psychology must be heeded. The complex relations between depth psychology as an intuitive, internalizing, archaeological discipline and mass psychology as an empirical, statistical, externalizing, teleological discipline must be investigated—the two models are not homologous, and the specific terms of their interaction are yet to be established. (And we must be on constant guard against those aspects of film theory which are but a projection of the theoretician's psychological particularities onto the theoretical field, or a projection of theoretical conceits into the filmic analysis.) In terms of our present analysis, this means that to speak of *a spectator* or *an audience* would imply totally different hermeneutic paradigms.

Yet the notion of a sheer positioning of the subject according to this complex of Oedipal possibilities is in itself a too abstract and descriptively insufficient determinant of ego formation and spectatorial positioning. The two major modes of imaginary spectatorial positioning within the scenarization of phantasms embodied and disembodied must be taken into account. (1) The disembodied phantasmatic variation: the self is fantasized as one of the three characters in the scene, thus it is a primal scene *à trois*, in which the subject plays an observed, represented role; (2) The embodied phantasmatic variation: the self observes the scene, thus it is a primal scene *à deux*, in which the subject plays the unrepresented role of the observor. We can either *see ourselves seeing the scene* or *see the scene*. Thus there exists a structural ambiguity possible on the level of spectatorial position as well as on the level of identification.

Yet further complications exist in regard to the mode of scenarization itself. The primal scene may be represented in either nocturnal dreams or diurnal fantasies, in psychotic deliria or in the symbolic structures of neurotic behavior. Thus it may appear in either literal (scenarized) or symbolic (iconic or symptomatic) form. In the literal mode, identification and subject position are manifestly apparent. In the symbolic mode, subject identification and position are patently complex, often dissimulated from the subject, and may be determined according to the two basic paradigms of subject construction within Freudian metapsychology: the model of the dreamwork, where any and indeed every figure may represent the self[10]; the model of the body as a paradigmatic symbolic system, upon which and according to which desire may be scenarized: "The ego is first and foremost a bodily ego; it is not merely a surface entity, but is itself the projection of a surface."[11] (This is also central to the phenomenological epistemology of the lived-body in its relation to the cultural realm; Merleau-Ponty explains that the body, "is that strange object which uses its own parts as a general system of symbols for the world."[12]) The delineation of these differences will permit us to consider an extreme example of the symbolization of the primal scene upon the body, which in turn may serve as the foundation for a critical hermeneutic of spectatorship.

In the work of the psychoanalyst Sami-Ali, we find a case of depersonalization in which this problematic takes a most radical turn.[13] This case history (which is so complex that readers must refer to the original text for the complete details) reveals how the ambiguities of the primal scene are symbolically lived through on the erotic surface of the body. It also shows how this scenarization reveals the disjunctions of the libidinal cathexes that determine the egological, identificatory, and spectatorial positioning of the subject. The essential features of the case are as follows: The anguish of the patient, Agnès, stems from the fact that she can no longer recognize herself, can no longer live through a stable identity. The psychotherapeutic situation revealed that "the role playing was as labile as the corporeal sensations, which denoted the narcissistic nature of this multiplicity, Agnès being *all* of the characters in which she projected herself."[14] Apparent in many of the phantasms which she recounts—all of which are interpreted by Sami-Ali to be variations on the primal scene—this multiplicity is most evidently manifested in one emblematic dream: "Bearing a penis the size of a bull's, Agnès makes love with a woman, without being embarrassed by the presence of a little girl. She feels a nearly orgasmic pleasure which causes her to awaken. The dreamer is here simultaneously the father who possesses the penis, the child who watches, and the mother who has an orgasm."[15] Whence the ambiguity of identification, where the primary process rules the determinations of libidinal cathexes and reorganizes the restraints of Oedipal repression and ego formation. In the phenomenon of depersonalization, the limits of the ego are transgressed, and the self/other distinction is erased (as is also often the case in schizophrenia.)

But in depersonalization not only is self-identification thrown into an ambiguous transfer and confusion of personalities—the body also becomes the place on which the primal scene is symbolically replayed. In the case of Agnès, witnessing a primal scene where the mother and father seemed to become one single creature led to the confusion of her own erotic topoi. Thus we find, in her phantasms, the equivalence on the one part between mouth, vagina, and anus, and on the other part between penis, finger, clitoris, and breast.[16] Of interest is both how this unleashing of the combinatory and identificatory possibilities of the primary process surmounts the Oedipal restrictions on classic iconography, as well as the manner in which the scenarization of desire may create an ambiguous situation in regard to the subject's spectatorial position and mechanisms of desire. It is precisely within the polysemy, the polyvalence, of these figurations that we shall discover the critical implications of this case history (just as a similarly ambiguous "egology" determines the radical significance of Hollis Frampton's film *Poetic Justice*).[17]

Surrealism has already revealed the iconographic possibilities of this sort of sexual inmixing, this sort of metaphoric condensation or substitution of erotic organs. Witness, on both the pictorial and the theoretical level, Salvador Dali's paranoic-critical method, as well as Lacan's investigations of pictorial representations and distortions, closely allied with Dali's work.[18] Or, for example, there is a close analogy between Agnès' corporeal ambiguities and conflations and Magritte's painting

Le viol, where a female torso is transformed into a face—the groin serves as mouth, the navel as nose, and the nipples as eyes. Hans Bellmer's drawings and his text *La petite anatomie de l'image* are also of related interest. These works, as well as Agnès' own description of her physical "iconography," depict not a regression to the polymorphous perversity of infantile sexuality, but an adult, perverse inmixing of oral, anal, and genital modes of sexuality within one ambiguous, polyvalent system. Her regression bears with it all posterior erotic modes: the repressive, limiting erotic organization of the Oedipal complex is not overcome, but merely overlayed with pre- and post-Oedipal modes of eroticism. The entire set of erotic possibilities of the symbolic corporeal combinatory system are actualized, entailing gender confusion and a consequent confusion of identity.

Yet Agnès' ambiguous mode of identification was not restricted to either the subject, her body, or to her phantasms of the Oedipal primal scene. As might be expected—according to the transferential exigencies of the therapeutic situation—this ambiguity was also projected upon the person of the psychotherapist. The libidinized *acting out* resulted in a similar ambiguity in regard to the identity of the psychotherapist who, according to the particularities of these phantasmatic transformations, was posited as either woman, man, or man/woman (androgyne).[19] The manifestation of the primal scene is but a projection of corporeal contradictions onto the phantasmatic scenario.[20] The multiple identifications and polyvalent erotic combinations specific to depersonalization are a sign of narcissistic plenitude, determining a coincidence of subject and object, inside and outside, passive and active, self and other.[21] What would constitute a cure is the move toward libidinal unity (Oedipalization), whereby the disjunctive libidinal cathexes and symbolic formations would be integrated into a given type of love-object, thereby coalescing and limiting the subject's identificatory patterns. Thus the acting out or working through of depersonalization reveals the contradictory origins of the self to be a function not only of desire, but also of the erotic activity of the other(s).

Acting out, in psychoanalytic terminology, signifies the "manifestation, in a new situation, of behaviour appropriate to an earlier situation, with the new situation symbolically representing the earlier one."[22] In a sense, it reveals the transformation of the self, a mode of becoming other. And it is of particular psychotherapeutic importance in regard to the transferential situation in analysis, where the upsurge of impulsive (and a fortiori symbolic) repetitive acts is meshed with the transferential dynamic. Such acts performed under the impetus of the analytic situation and its emotional imperatives, may in fact be accomplished either within or outside of the analytic situation. Freud maintains that such "abnormal" acts must occur solely within analysis, and that outside of analysis they should be relegated to recollection, if the meaning of such acting out is to be ascertained, and the movement toward a cure effected. It is such working through that often produces the extreme representations of the primal scene in analysis, precisely because of the encouragement to act, and act out in the extreme—rather than merely remember—the repressed material. In acting out, the repressed or the disavowed returns neither as psychotic delirium, neurotic symbol, nor hysterical gesture, but as action, and can thus be "managed" within the analytical scenario. Such "management"—a movement toward the cure, toward a sort of normalization—entails a staging of the patient's phantasm. It is precisely for this reason that Freud, in his case history cited above, felt that in retelling the tale he could change the scene but must retain the details: the specifics of the ulterior or manifest scene are of little import, since in all cases, according to Freud, the scene is derived from, reduced to, the primal scene. Orthodox psychoanalysis thus reduces the particularities of the analytic situation to a unitary Oedipal structure. The acting out in its "abnormal" relation to everyday life is in fact structured according to the stereotypicality of the unconscious (the transformative possibilities of which are already revealed as the condition of psychic representability, as explained in *The Interpretation of Dreams*). Thus while the specifics of acting out may differ from case to case, their meaning is reduced to the anterior text (script) of the primal scene, read according to a master hermeneutic text (i.e., psychoanalytic metapsychology). Though the narrative may differ, the dénouement is always restricted to a narrow field of possibilities (see the combinatory of permutations of "I love him" listed above) within the even narrower categorizations of the cure (i.e., the elimination of compulsive acts) or the continuation of the illness (i.e., the continuation of such acts). The "acting" of acting out maintains its scenarized specificity only as a symbolic manifestation of the unconscious processes determined by the reactions to the Oedipal complex, to the primal scene.

In the analytic situation, acting out entails a mode of derealization, insofar as this scenarization sustains an effective emotional and gestural break with everyday existence. This rupture, within the context of the transferential situation, brings to consciousness repressed material of the primal scene, upon which the entire basis of personality and propriate organization is founded. Thus the transference is a mode of identification with the origins of the subject, origins which were repressed due to the narcissistic wounds they entailed. The pain of analysis is caused by reopening these wounds, entailing the even greater difficulty of discovering that the self is based upon a wound, a rupture, a violence, a lack. Analysis opens these wounds in order to review the originary (primal) situation, with the goal of reorganizing or rearticulating the personality.

These lessons should not be lost on aesthetics. As *acting out* is in part a function of psychic *derealization* within the psychotherapeutic process, conversely it might be said that in mainstream cinema *acting* is a function of *realism,* or of a realist ontology. In the psychotherapeutic situation, acting out is a direct symbolic representation of an earlier situation, articulated by the threshold of repression; in mainstream Hollywood cinema, acting is also the directed, staged reproduction of an earlier scene, the written scenario. (Acting, in certain rare instances, can also be acting out, as in the case of the extreme manifestation of character acting by someone like Artaud.) But in cinema, such acting is a literal, and not a symbolic, representation of the script, always available to conscious representations and manipulations.[23] This sets the scene for the conditions of verisimilitude upon which mainstream cinema is founded, and upon which normative modes of spectatorial identification are based. (As with numerous comparisons between psychic and cinematic structures, these relations—between acting and acting out, in regard to actor, patient and spectator—are metaphoric or analogical, and not causal. Thus the parallels discussed here are to be understood in their function as representations or constructs; if certain cinematic structures reveal the topology of consciousness and/or the lineaments of the unconscious, it is quite simply because all expression necessarily does so. We must avoid the category errors inherent in the inappropriate homologization of psychotherapeutic procedures and film theory. Film is not a phantasm; the movie-goer is not a patient; the cinematic apparatus is not the psychic apparatus: all parallels thereof must be explained within their proper hermeneutic limits, and the epistemological trap based on resemblance must be avoided.)

André Bazin explains that, "At the source of the disenchantment which follows the film one could doubtless detect a process of depersonalization of the spectator."[24] In the cinema understood as mass identificatory mechanism, the spectator identifies primarily with the film's hero: the depersonalization which obtains is a function of the partial loss of self within this identificatory process; the disenchantment is a function of the "conflict of realities," between the filmed world and the real world outside the cinema hall. Thus it is due precisely to the realist paradigm—prejudice—of mainstream narrative cinema that spectatorial depersonalization occurs as part of the cinematic experience. Yet the difference between this type of depersonalization and that of the psychotherapeutic procedure must be noted: in the filmic experience, there is primarily a passive identification with the hero, and an extremely minimal "acting out" upon leaving the theater. Conversely, in the psychotherapeutic experience there is primarily an active identification/transference with the analyst/Oedipal figure, along with a maximum of acting out. In relation to the cinema, there is, concurrent with identification, a relatively great degree of self-consciousness (and consciousness of the film as external event), with the ratio of identification/depersonalization to self-consciousness varying according to each spectator's psychic threshold for identification, pleasure, fixation, depersonalization, etc. This ratio is the very "conflict at the heart of identification," a struggle between identification and alienation, between depersonalization and self-consciousness.[25] This is certainly also the case in psychotherapy, with the major difference being that self-consciousness is not presupposed, but is precisely what is to be developed through the utilization of depersonalization in acting out; in the process of aesthetic spectatorship this occurs only minimally.

In psychotherapy—unlike film spectatorship, which is a one-sided affair—there is a dialectical relation of desire/identification/alienation between analyst and analysand; this obviously cannot occur between a film's spectator and its hero. As Émile Benveniste has shown in regard to the linguistic functions of interpersonal relations and communication, the linguistic foundation of dynamic subjectivity is a function of the dialectic between "I" and "you," the reality of the world is insinuated into this relation through the third, more static, objective function of "he," "she," and "it."[26] In psychoanalytic terms, this dialectic is the dialectic of desire, whereby the subject is constituted.[27] Psychoanalysis is the articulation and organization of *personality*; cinema is the articulation and organization of *persona*. In the classical Hollywood narrative film, desire—i.e., the desires of the film's personages—is alternately defeated and fulfilled within the scenario, where the artificial ordering of the subject effects the veritable closure of the narrative process, its "suture." Unlike classic theatrical tragedy, cinematic catharsis is not essentially a function of identification leading to sorrow and pity, but rather a function of the modalities and exigencies of desire. Yet for the film spectator, this desire is perpetually unanswered and consequently reverberates with narcissistic responses. The scenarization of the filmic text elicits and guides spectatorial desire—at least that of a certain proportion of viewers, since there are always others who are left cold—but it never responds. In relation to the spectator, there is no interlocutory "you" in the film—all film characters exist in the grammatical mode of the third person (identificatory desires and phantasms notwithstanding).

In cinematic acting, there is an intertwining of stereotypicality and specificity, founded upon the differences between the actor's persona and the characteristics demanded of the personage by the script and the director. As in any mode of representation, the degree and type of stereotyping is determined by historical conditions of representability. This is precisely why, for example, most acting styles become dated. Conversely, the specificity of acting is a function of the actor's particularities, peculiarities, idiosyncrasies—the actor's style. Neither such acting stereotypes nor the actor's style are reducible to the script, the scenario; and such peculiarities (individualities) indeed arrange a certain set of connotations as deviations from the script. The script's meaning is inflected by persona and performance, by the divergences that distinguish the *persona* and the *person* of the actor.

The value and significance of acting in any hermeneutic of the cinema is a function of the interpretive model, the epistemology, upon which the hermeneutic system is founded. It is in fact no accident that popular film criticism is primarily founded upon considerations of acting and verisimilitude, while most contemporary academic, theoretical film writing tends to shun major considerations of acting, leaving this to theater studies, sociology, anthropology, and film production. This divergence may be accounted for by the differences between the two major hermeneutic paradigms in film studies: the phenomenological/realist and the metapsychological/ structuralist models. Most contemporary popular film criticism is founded upon the former; current theoretical film theory, to a great extent, is founded upon the latter. In terms of the function of acting, this difference is noteworthy. In the phenomenological model, acting (as gesture) is considered to be a prime cause in the production of cinematic effects of verisimilitude, of realism. Indeed, even the briefest perusal of a phenomenological text such as Maurice Merleau-Ponty's *Phenomenology of Perception* will reveal how gesture serves as the central, and ontologically primal, paradigm of meaning and communication. This is effected to such an extent that in this work speech itself is ultimately reduced to a mode of gesture, and expression is based on a corporeal paradigm. In Emmanuel Levinas's phenomenology, especially as expressed in *Totality and Infinity*, this paradigm entails the consideration of subjectivity itself as a gestural effect.[28]

Conversely, in theories based on Freudian metapsychology, acting is considered to be an effect of subjectivity. Consider Stephen Heath's claim that "the subject-reflection is a narrative effect," and that, "All presentation, however, is representation—a production, a construction of positions and effects—and all representation is performance—the time of that production and construction, of the realization of positions and effects."[29] In the psychotherapeutic situation, the gestures of acting out are effects, symptoms, whose meaning is a function of the situatedness of the acting subject within the Oedipal milieu, the Oedipal narrative. In the metaphyschological theorization of the cinema, the status of acting is also that of a narrative effect, whose meaning is a function of narratological construction. (This parallels the Hegelian and Marxist dialectical epistemologies, where gesture as meaningful effect is already predetermined by the historical development of the subject. Thus it is entirely appropriate that Lacanian metapsychology should rely on Hegel as a metaphysical base, and that the dominant trend in contemporary film theory should be founded upon a combination of Freudian and Marxist epistemologies.) In short, popular film criticism (with its positivist/realist prejudices) deals with acting as the key to characterological identity; conversely, most film theory does not consider acting to be of prime importance precisely due to the theoretical prejudice in favor of distantiation both of the Brechtian and the psychopathological sort.

In both psychotherapy and cinema spectatorship, the operative structural modification in the process of identification and desire is the depersonalization arising from a splitting of the ego. This splitting is an ego-defense mechanism which, on the aesthetic level, establishes the ego as an otherness in the text; the partial loss of self in identification entails the creation of alterity on the basis of ego disturbances, as a sort of analytic of the ego. The cure (interiorly) and the filmic text (exteriorly) are propadeutic procedures whose metatexts (the Oedipal scenario or the film's narrative script) provide the formations of the synthesis of the ego. Subjectivity is here determined by the dialectic between such an analysis and synthesis, between the conditions which split the ego and those which would effect its (re)integration. For the patient in psychotherapy this might actually occur, while for the film spectator this synthesis remains a distant representation on screen, the object of at best a wishful "projection"—that of the projector and the spectator!—thus ultimately an alienating effect.

In terms of the representation of the psychological constitution of film characters, such ego integration is an a priori of the text in mainstream narrative cinema; within the psychoanalytic "script" (i.e., in analysis), it remains as merely an idealized goal. In this regard, the major differences between cinematic acting and therapeutic acting out are apparent: acting in the cinema is ultimately subordinate to the script; acting out in therapy is, rather, a sort of insubordination, an ultimately futile attempt to escape the confines, determinations, and restrictions of the Oedipal, familial script.

Regarding the subject-function and narrative in the cinema, Stephen Heath rightly observes that in the avant-garde cinema there is "a threat translated in the common reactions of 'boredom,' the irritation of 'nothing happens'—a great deal happens, of course, but not the performance of 'the subject.' "[30] It is precisely this cinematic voiding of narration and subject construction which permits the advent of a "theoretical cinema," a cinema of ideas, a cinema which may serve as allegory for theoretical positions and psychological states, as is the case for Godard, Frampton, Snow and many others. (Note, as Heath also points out, that narrative film may also produce these effects, but in a quite different fashion.)

In a film such as Hollis Frampton's *Poetic Justice* (where the only images are the written pages of a scenario, stacking up one-by-one on a table, to be read by the spectator), the particularities of acting, style, and identificatory presence are eliminated, or at least made fully ambiguous and open to the spectator's projective mechanisms.[31] The stylistic specificity of acting and the determinations of persona are effaced in a universalized—or at least generalized—indetermination, structured by the utilization of linguistic shifters. (Thus we *read* the narrator's voice speaking of "you" and "your lover," terms which pertain to everyone and no one, since their reference changes with each reader and each reading. Due to its own mode of iconic suppression of characteristic detail, *Poetic Justice* is a truly universalized filmic text, permitting any mode of identification according to our combinatory of contingent psychic states and positions.) This film may be understood as yet one more scenarization of the primal scene (in one sequence we read that "Your lover's hand is holding a still photograph of myself, filming you and your lover.")[32] It maintains a full ambiguity of identificatory possibilities, permitting the eventuality of an active derealization and depersonalization in regard to the cinematic apparatus. This certainly does not preclude it from being overdetermined as the scenarization of other syndromes (such as voyeurism) and other texts. This film serves as a hermeneutic—and not a therapeutic—device.

We, the spectators, may insinuate ourselves into the cinematic scenarization of *Poetic Justice* in several possible imaginary ways: (1) as an exterior spectator who imagines two people making love watched by a third person (i.e., as a disembodied spectator); (2) in total identification with the person who is watching the two others making love (i.e., as an embodied spectator); (3) in total identification with one of the lovers (i.e., as an embodied participant); or (4) in partial identification with any or all of the people in the scene (i.e., as an embodied but fragmented spectator/participant.)

Furthermore, for each of these possibilities, the character and spectator may be construed/constructed as either male or female, heterosexual, homosexual, or bisexual.[33] Thus there is a complete indetermination of sexual identity and object choice, as well as an open-ended scenarization of the primal scene. The specific commutation of terms is maximally determined by the phantasms which guide each different spectator's psychic activity, and minimally determined by the narrative course of filmic events. Of course, if the Oedipal complex is indeed a universal determinant of psychological formation and ontogenesis, then every tale would somehow be a variant of this originary phantasm. Whether or not this is the case, *Poetic Justice* more specifically provides an exemplary scenario of such triangular interpersonal relations, all the while suggesting an expanded abstract model of spectatorial identification for all cinema. It provides an abstract, empty parallel for the Freudian combinatory of identificatory presence, *without* any specific psychosexual ramifications.

In terms of film spectatorship, the implied spectator is an ideal spectator; but the ideal seldom coincides with the empirical. This is assuredly an asymmetrical relationship insofar as the two egos—psychological/empirical and ideal/transcendental—do not coincide in either their origins, formations, or effects. In the filmic text, the ideal ego of the implied spectator is abstractly constructed according to narrative and iconic functions (though in *Poetic Justice* there is a notable paucity of iconicity). The empirical ego of the spectator(s) may only be coincidentally congruous with this ideal ego. (Here, the degree of identification depends upon the degree of coincidence, of congruence, or of desire.) Whence the hermeneutic difference at stake in this discussion. While every scenarization proffers an ideal mode of reading the text (an "ideal reader"), reading ultimately tends toward what Umberto Eco refers to as to "aberrant decoding," which entails the central problem of any universalizing hermeneutic procedure.[34] The very existence of the possibility of interpretation implies that this ideal escapes the empirical conditions of readership—ultimately, every reading is aberrant. In this regard, as Roland Barthes eloquently explains: "The novel is in effect a faked mathesis, leading to a misappropriation [*détournement*] of knowledge."[35] But while the relation between the ideal and the empirical is asymmetric, it is nevertheless reciprocal: the narrative function sets the limits of identificatory possibility; the "mind-set" of the psychological ego sets the limits of spectatorial projection into the narrative—the experience of narrative cinema is a function of the overlap of these two patterns.

We now discover the inner structural formation which justifies Marcel Duchamp's claim that the artwork is completed by the spectator: the intertwining of the (cinematically represented) ideal ego with the spectator's empirical ego—i.e., the intertwining of the subject implied by the narrative with the real viewing subject—determines the "dialectic" between artwork and spectator. The artwork serves as an identificatory commutation because it motivates the splitting of the ego and the setting up of that split ego in the text as alterity. This is true for both artist and spectator. Thus the artist's intention is a necessary condition for producing the work, but knowledge of this intention is never a sufficient condition for viewing the work, since in viewing it the spectator's ego (each and every different spectator's ego) is also split and reinstated in the work. This situation is a fortiori true of *Poetic Justice*: we have shown in a previous study how this film is a function of Frampton's ego-defense in regard to a certain anxiety of influence;[36] in the present text we discover this film's manifold possibilities of spectatorial identification.

Yet we must not forget that *Poetic Justice*, whatever its force, is most certainly a cinematic oddity—an iconoclastic film. But perhaps it is only through such a hermeneutic iconoclasm that we may reveal the iconophilia of our own phantasms, an iconophilia on which mainstream narrative cinema thrives. In the avant-garde limit of sublimation posited by *Poetic Justice*, do we not find, perhaps, the manner in which universal reason actually does refer back to the individual? Are we not projected out onto theoretical speculation, precisely because of the lack of psychic identification? Does not iconophobia give rise to a new iconophilia?

8   lucid intervals:
postmodernism and
photography

About all that is left, in each case, is an archetypal fragment of living action, potentially subject to the incessant reiteration that is one of the most familiar and intolerable features of our dreams.

—Hollis Frampton

Michel Tournier's brilliant short story, "Veronica's Shrouds," is a reworking of Poe's "The Oval Portrait" in relation to the photographic signifier.[1] This is the tale of the photographer Veronica and her model Hector. Struck by his beauty, she takes him in charge so as to make him *photogenic*, thus surpassing the mere physical beauty of the real object. Her cares to this end result in the decline of his physical beauty and health. Yet Veronica is not satisfied with the results. Influenced by the deliberate capture of eternity in the photographs of Edward Weston, she notes that aesthetic advances in life studies were mainly due to the discovery of the corpse as an anatomical model. She thus wishes to photograph corpses in a morgue, desiring to produce a true still life, a *nature morte*, images literally *taken from life.* Morbidly, but coherently, she insists on the move from dissection to vivisection as the guarantee of authenticity! From these observations she creates a new mode of photography: the *direct photo.* Wishing to surpass the technical constraints of her art, she produces "photographs" without camera, film, or enlarger, by exposing large sheets of photographic paper to the light, then having her model, dipped in developing fluid, lie on the paper, which when fixed creates life-size silhouettes—much like those left on the pavements at Hiroshima, projections of the bodies of people

119

vaporized by the blast of the atomic bomb. Needless to say, this artistic progress severely accelerates the physical decline of Hector, whose body is covered with the worst erythema, lesions due to the chemical action of the developing fluid. The final step is not far away. Veronica finally surpasses photography itself by creating *dermography*: linen made light-sensitive by impregnation with silver bromide is wrapped around her model's chemically soaked body; when fixed and unfolded this creates a sort of funeral frieze, similar to the famed Shroud of Turin—"Veronica's Shrouds." Her ultimate work coincides with her model's death: in her art she achieves her wish to change the object itself.

The death of the subject transforms the subject into object and permits its assumption as sign. If, as Roland Barthes claims, photography is "the dead theater of Death, the foreclosure of the Tragic; it excludes all purification, all *catharsis*,"[2] the photograph is nevertheless but a sign of death; Veronica's shrouds, to the contrary, transform the simulacrum into the real. Death is not signified, but caused, by the artistic object. Veronica's shrouds become a bizarre instrument of Walter Benjamin's desire to politicize art, of Barthes's desire to change the object itself.

The metaphysical poignancy of this tale is well expressed by a remark about the photographic signifier made by Philippe Dubois: what is at stake is "the impossibility of having the real coincide with its representation."[3] In fact, every depth hermeneutic is bound to this pathos. This explains the extreme fascination with one's own portrait: as Barthes understands so well, the portrait is a sign of the inevitable death of the subject, thus the portrait is in fact a sort of *nature morte* which might well pass into eternity, while the sitter never will. Hence photography's depressing vampirism, and the hidden pathos of the family snapshot.

Such pathos is not an attribute of postmodernist art. Indeed, it is a sign of the continuation of the romantic—and even the classical—tradition within modernism itself. Thus the pathos of tragic modernist irony—which overdetermines the codes of postmodernism—is transfigured into parody in the postmodernist work. In a sense, postmodernism entails the ironization of irony, achieved by making explicit the rhetorical and iconic forms of modernist art. In postmodernism's ideal limit, tragedy and parody are conflated in a new form of criticism. But it would seem, ultimately, that even such criticism itself will be assimilated in a more general textuality and iconography where it will disappear into a "universal" magma of signs, lost in the flux of history.

In this context, the apparent tautologies, stating that the representation is not the real and the signifier is not the signified, take on critical importance. Postmodernist epistemology, especially in Jean Baudrillard's model which we will consider, entails precisely the conflation of representation and reality, resulting in the inherent loss of (political) pathos and the failure of the modernist utopian project. Perhaps utopia needs tragedy as its mainspring, and perhaps postmodernist irony, cynicism, and apathy indeed find a major precursor in Marcel Duchamp's "aesthetic indifference" and "ironic causality." But in any case, we must be prepared to include the postmodernist work itself in a *mise-en-abîme* of aesthetic signifiers, and avoid considering postmodernism as the telos of modernist art.

The photographic pathos or tragedy is determined by the hermeneutic incommensurability of signifier and signified, surface and depth, image and referent. Modernism searches for this coherence in the depths of hidden phantasms; postmodernism manifests this coherence on the very surface of the artwork, produced as the referential purity (emptiness) of the simulacrum. Veronica's shrouds thus present the tragic irony of modernism from which postmodernism arises: the creation of the artwork always entails the "death of the subject." It would be too much to hope that the death of the spectator is not close at hand. For photography, that popular art, is the universalization of *vanitas*, where only the sophistry of criticism will discover Utopia.

The theorization of the visual image within the postmodernist debate finds its ontological/epistemological foundation in the theory of simulacra, notably in the version presented by Baudrillard. We will contrast Baudrillard's version to the quite different theory of simulacra proposed by Pierre Klossowski, with the intent of distinguishing between surface and depth hermeneutics, so as to examine the aesthetic variations and incommensurabilities of these two positions, and discuss their implications for a theory of postmodernist photography.

Klossowski, citing Hermes Trismegistus, explains the ancient origins of the notion of the simulacrum by revealing its inherent aesthetic of fascination and visual pleasure, and the concommitant "bodily solicitation of the viewer by the picture."[4] This solicitation is effected because the idol is the *simulacrum* of a god, an object in which the soul of a god or angel is enclosed, giving these idols and images the power of good and evil. Klossowski deems himself a creator of such simulacra, explaining that in fact the demons invoked by his artworks are merely "hypostases of active obsessional forces."[5] In uneasy conformity with modern depth psychology, the ancient gods are homologous with modern obsessions—as when Artaud insists that "God is the monomaniac of the unconscious." On the psychological level, Klossowski explains that, "The simulacrum in its *imitative* sense is the actualization of something in itself incommunicable and unrepresentable: properly speaking, it is the phantasm in its obsessional constraint."[6] These obsessions, operating differently but simultaneously in the artist and the viewer (two differently coded systems, of production and reception respectively), are the origins of simulacra. The simulacrum as representation transforms the inner phantasms into conventional and institutional stereotypes. Following Nietzsche's definition of truth, Klossowski defines simulacra and stereotypes: "In effect, at the level of linguistic expression as well as plastic figuration, stereotypes are only the residues of phantasmatic simulacra fallen into current usage, abandoned to common interpretation."[7]

This is a fortiori true of the photographic image: we might remember that in French the word *cliché* means both photograph and stereotype. Klossowski, following received opinion, understands photography to be a causal factor in the rise of modernist art; the appropriation of the figurative process by photography motivated the abandonment of the subject in painting—"The painting ceases to be a simulacrum in order to become an [object] in-itself."[8] Echoing Benjamin's observations in the "The Work of Art in the Age of Mechanical Reproduction" (which, not coincidentally, was translated into French by Klossowski), Klossowski writes that, "After photography, the cinema will, all the more so, 'liberate painting from the need to imitate nature.' "[9] This would seem to obviate the cathartic effect of the simulacrum. Aesthetic catharsis, for Klossowski, consists in ridding the artist of the phantasm's obsessional constraint, only to instill it anew in the viewer. Thus the simulacrum is understood according to a depth hermeneutics of representation (phantasm/simulacra) which operates as a structure of exchange (artist/viewer). Catharsis, for Klossowski, operates on a psychological/theological model; despite his antimodernist fears of the loss of the subject in art, despite his figurative artistic production, and despite his other protestations to the contrary, his theoretical stance remains one of high modernism, even while his pictorial production attempts an anachronistic classicism. Klossowski's work, in all its manifestations, escapes the "postmodernist" temptation.

For Benjamin, the photographic image (or simulacrum) entails the dissolution of artistic "aura," and inaugurates the possibility of the political use of the image. As such, catharsis can no longer be understood according to a personalist psychological model, and must now be grasped in a political, revolutionary model. Discussing the relations between mechanical reproduction and mass movements, he explains that: "Their most powerful agent is the film. Its social significance, particularly in its most positive form, is inconceivable without its destructive, cathartic aspect, that is, the liquidation of the traditional value of the cultural heritage."[10] By releasing art from ritual and endowing it with a political usage, aesthetics now enters the realm of political idealist utopianism, veiled by Benjamin as dialectical materialism. Yet that one final, social catharsis is necessary for this effect; if this is to be a mass catharsis, it is no surprise that it will be effected through the most commonplace stereotypes, in the most appropriate medium for that end—the cinema. (Where Klossowski sees the end of cathartic possibilities, Benjamin sees the final transformation of catharsis in an apocalyptic political upheavel.) This new reign of photographic and cinematic simulacra entails a radical epistemological break: "Thus is manifested in the field of perception what in the theoretical sphere is noticeable in the increasing importance of statistics."[11]

This position is in marked contrast with Baudrillard's notion of simulacra, where catharsis no longer exists and where the "euphoria of simulation" is free from the "anguish of the referential."[12] For Baudrillard, the generation of simulacra is no longer a function of referentiality or phantasmagoria: "It is the generation by models of a real without origin or reality: the hyperreal."[13] The simulacrum is thus opposed to representation; it is the radical negation of the sign as exchange value. Its ontological status is defined according to diverse (and, according to Baudrillard, historically successive) phases of the *image,* defined as that which "(1) reflects a profound reality; (2) masks and denatures a profound reality; (3) masks the *absence* of any profound reality; and (4) is without relation to any reality whatsoever; it is its own pure simulacrum."[14]

What is of concern here, as the crucial ontological question of the simulacrum, is precisely where we are to establish the epistemological cut. To make it between phase 2 and phase 3 would be to remain within metaphysics; to make it between phase 3 and phase 4 would be to take the deconstructive position whereby metaphysics is not overcome, but is rather presented as a particular discursive possibility which happens to be at the foundations of our culture, according to which all else must be read, but which is nevertheless a fiction, a model of reality. As such, the simulacral entails the loss of reference in the media of a mass culture, and the absorption of the social into the statistical. Representation (on both the aesthetic and the political model) is no longer possible. Fascination is a function of neutralizing meaning in favor of the idol and truth in favor of simulacra.[15] (Representational theory entails the generation of models by reality; simulacral theory entails the generation of reality by models.) Both rationality and meaningful dialectic (as well as any "master narrative") are rejected.

> They are given meaning: they want spectacle. No effort has been able to convert them to the seriousness of the content, nor even to the seriousness of the code. Messages are given to them, they only want some sign, they idolise the play of signs and stereotypes, they idolise any content so long as it resolves itself into a spectacular sequence.[16]

In an earlier work, Baudrillard describes the central structural features of hyperreal simulation (i.e., phase 4 of the image):[17] (1) the deconstruction of the real in its details; the paradigmatic declension of the object; the flattening, linearity, and seriality of partial objects; (2) the doubling and multiplication of objects in a *vision-en-abîme*, which is ultimately another type of seriality, where the real is no longer reflected, but rather exhausted in its own involution; (3) the abolition of both the syntagmatic and paradigmatic dimensions in a properly serial form, fully without reflexion; the infinite generation of forms by models; the infinite diffraction of the object within itself; (4) the generative form is not of pure repetition, but rather of minimal differences which differentiate the various terms; hence this is a mode of digitality, not representation.

It is striking how these characteristics describe—in a markedly avant-garde mode—the photographic and especially the cinematic signifiers, those foundations of our age of mechanical reproduction. We cannot help seeing the "euphoria of simulation" as homologous with the visual pleasure generated by the cinematic apparatus.[18] Yet we must contrast the realist and the hyperrealist—the representational and the simulacral—models of cinema. André Bazin's *realist* ontology of the cinema—advocating the telos of cinema as the ultimate *Gesamtkunstwerk,* the ultimate representation of reality—saw film as the ontological closure of art, where the cinematic machine is dissimulated by the very illusion its produces, in order to heighten the impression of reality.[19] To the contrary, Baudrillard's *hyperrealist* ontology of simulacra—relying on a cybernetic model in which artwork and machine are interchangeable signs—is nothing less than a cinematic delusion of the real as an endless projection of copies, an "aesthetic hallucination of reality." We are accustomed to the commonplace notion that modernism was the result of the encroachment of photographic reproduction on the artistic field; we may now note another commonplace—also proclaimed by Benjamin and thematized by Baudrillard, among others—that cinema's encroachment on the artistic field, and especially the invasion of "high" art by "popular" art, is the foundational event of postmodernism.

Writing of the differences between modernism and postmodernism, Craig Owens explains: "Postmodernism neither brackets nor suspends the referent but works instead to problematize the activity of reference. When the postmodernist work speaks of itself, it is no longer to proclaim its autonomy, its self-sufficiency, its transcendence; rather, it is to narrate its own contingency, insufficiency, lack of transcendence."[20] According to this definition of modernism in terms of autonomy and transcendence, we might consider Michael Snow's film *La région centrale* (1970–71) as a high point of modernist art. The scenario is of minimal simplicity—approximately three hours of views of a purely natural mountain scene, describing a day and night, with the camera rotating on a special machine which permitted it any possible camera angle, rotation movement, rotation speed, and focal length, making it a sort of truly panoptical cinematic device. The sophistication of the cinematic machine belies the utter simplicity of the iconography, which varies from figurative to abstract according to the speed of camera movement and degree of natural lighting. The result of this vacillation between figuration and abstraction, caused by an excessive, unhuman (mechanical) motion, is that of extreme vertigo, the metaphysical implications of which are described by Annette Michelson: "Snow's infinitely mobile framing, his mimesis of and gloss upon spatial exploration offer, most importantly, a fusion of primary scopophilic and epistemophilic impulses in the cinematic rendering of the grand metaphor of the transcendental subject."[21] It is precisely as a hyperbolic instantiation emblematic of the transcendental ego that this film is a prime example of modernist art, where the transcendental ego—a metaphoric transformation of the cinematic apparatus—becomes the implied *"auteur"* of the filmic narrative. Yet *this* allegorical situation is hardly the case for the postmodernist condition.

Stressing the explicit contingency and lack of transcendence characteristic of postmodernist art, Owens ends the aforementioned article with a quotation from Barthes's seminal essay, "Change the Object Itself." This title is clearly a paraphrase of the eleventh of Marx's *Theses on Feuerbach:* "The philosophers have only *interpreted* the world in various ways; the point, however, is to *change* it." Hence Barthes's observation that, "It is no longer the myths which need to be unmasked . . . it is the sign itself which must be shaken," in order to "fissure the very representation of meaning," to "challenge the symbolic itself."[22] In fact, in regard to the problematic of the aesthetics of mechanical reproduction and catharsis, the autonomy of a pure, transcendental ego would have no need of catharsis; only the empirical, psychological ego, tainted by the impurities of contingent existence, needs catharsis to cleanse it of the anxieties wrought by history and the Other. The ideal(ist) spectator of modernist art is utopian; the ego of the postmodernist spectator is purely empirical: the previously utopian ideal is transformed into a dystopian parody. The wish to *change the object itself* evokes Benjamin's notion of the politicization of art; yet in Baudrillard's version of postmodernism, Benjamin's slight optimism is overcome by pessimism, or perhaps more correctly speaking by apathy, in which the very reality of the object itself is no longer of any concern, since all changes are on the level of the model which generates objects and reality. For Baudrillard, simulation is no longer a function of semiology. Yet if we are to investigate the transition from modernism to postmodernism, we must note how the semiological aspect of the object has been reworked and overcome; if the object as sign is to be changed, then semiology—the science of signs—must be evoked as the critical tool of such a task, as an objective leading to the postmodernist project of deconstructing semiology itself.

For Baudrillard, the ontological disparity between reality and representation, between signified and signifier, no longer obtains within the simulacrum. Simulacra are not, strictly speaking, signs. Thus we must investigate the ontological limits of signification, of signs, and determine precisely how simulacra can originate in a social field previously theorized as a nexus of signs and sign systems. The central question is whether the object of postmodern thought is a simulacrum whose operation is beyond signification—a sort of pure *pragma* without a determined task or goal; or whether it is an uncoded term within a vaster significative scene, a type of floating signifier generalized, universalized, made the norm instead of the exception. If the former is the case, then semiology itself becomes obsolete, just one more avatar of depth hermeneutics. If the latter case obtains, then the simulacrum may be understood as a new mutation in the significative field, a manifestation of an arational mode of production and communication. But perhaps both possibilities are simply theoretical constructs, and the simulacrum is merely the other side of the sign, apparent there where communication fails and where the social system cannot escape the stereotypes of its own ideology. Perhaps the simulacrum is the ironic reversal of the sign, just as postmodernism effects the appropriation and ironic—often carnivalesque—reversal of modernism.

Contemporary theory of the photographic sign (even within the context of postmodernism) relies heavily on C. S. Peirce's tripartite categorization of signs as *icon, symbol,* and *index.*[23] In relation to the aesthetic (photographic) modification of reality, these modes of signification correspond respectively to the *mirror* of the real, the *transformation* of the real, and the *trace* of the real. The photograph partakes of all three modalities of signification, and though it is usually praised for its extreme iconic (mimetic) possibilities, the iconic aspect is not essential to the photographic sign. Rather, its indexical nature (due to the chemical action of light on the film) is its essential characteristic. Peirce already noted the essentially indexical nature of the photograph in 1895; and it is this feature which grounds current theoretical research on the photographic sign—most notably the work of Rosalind Krauss and Philippe Dubois—in which a theoretical shift has occurred, from a theory of *mimesis* to a theory of *traces*.

Yet this pertains strictly to the *ontological* status of the photographic sign. Conversely, the *sociological* status of the photograph is that of a highly coded, indeed overcoded, entity. The photograph is caught in the intersection of two sets of codes: those of artistic composition and production *and* those of spectatorial aesthetic consumption, ruled by the systems of distribution and presentation. Only at the very instant of exposure can the photograph be deemed simply a pure trace; as a completed, presented work it is highly coded, and its meaning overdetermined by the multiple significative and social systems into which it is inserted or implicated. Hence Barthes's famous claim that the photograph is a "message without a code" is in fact inaccurate:[24] this condition obtains only at the split-second of exposure of the bare film, before the photograph exists as a visual entity. It is true of the latent image, never of the finished work. We must agree with Dubois that, as index, "the photographic image has no semantics other than its own pragmatics."[25] (This would almost seem to indicate that structurally the photograph is a priori a postmodernist aesthetic entity!). The photograph's pragmatics preceed its semantics, which is precisely the cause of what Barthes speaks of as its "Urdoxical" quality,[26] its peculiar mode of fascination, which in fact seems to reveal a new sort of aesthetic "aura." This quality is precisely the key to the "photographic impulse" (*pulsion photographique*[27]) which distinguishes photography from the other arts, be they mimetic, symbolic, or indexical. Yet as the photographic work is taken up into coded social systems, all three significative functions come into play in the constitution of its meaning. Thus to study this "change" in the photographic sign—to reveal its simulacral position within postmodern enunciation—we might consider several postmodernist works of photographic art which reveal the shifting emphases of iconic, symbolic, and indexical signification. This will disclose the very insufficiencies and ambiguities of the photographic signifier.

Perhaps the most radical work on the *indexical* function of the photographic sign is that of Sherrie Levine. Levine's most famous and controversial work consists in rephotographing the images of certain "modern masters" of photography. One example of this is the rephotogaphy, off a Witkin Gallery poster, of an Edward Weston photographic portrait of his son's nude torso. Discussing the possible infringement on copyright laws, Douglas Crimp explains the rights at stake here:

> I think, to be fair, however, we might just as well give them to Praxiteles, for if it is the *image* that can be owned, then surely these belong to classical sculpture, which would put them in the public domain. Levine has said that, when she showed her photographs to a friend, he remarked that they only made him want to see the originals. "Of course," she replied, "and the originals make you want to see that little boy, but when you see the boy, the art is gone." For the desire that is initiated by that representation does not come to closure around that little boy, is not at all satisfied by him. The desire of representation exists only insofar as it never be fulfilled, insofar as the original always be deferred. It is only in the absence of the original that representation may take place.[28]

This work's counterfeit aspect is a function of its iconic perfection, while its representational aspect is a function of its indexical complexity. Its singular value lies precisely in the difference between counterfeit and representation. The photograph—a meta-image, since it is printed from a negative image—is a fortiori simulacral. Levine's photograph is thus at least a third-order simulacrum (Levine—Witkin poster—Weston—Weston's son), with the potential interposition of an indefinite number of stylistically generative models. (We must differentiate between model and simulacrum). The referent of this photograph is lost in the world history of images and forms, while the photograph itself remains a thing among things. What is lost within this intertextual series of references is the authorial reference: while the authorship of the photograph-as-physical-object is never in question (it is Levine's, with whatever consequences of copyright infringement it may entail), the authorship of the photograph-as-semiological-object is always ambiguous and never resolvable. This work thus exemplifies the post-structuralist critique of transcendental egocentric subjectivity by making explicit the manner in which authorship is a social fiction, dependent upon the interplay of rhetorical/narrative structure and significative reference. While the classical (and modernist) artwork entails the construction of an ideal spectator and authorial presence, Levine's work, in a postmodern mode, entails the loss of the author and a confused spectatorial position. It is perhaps the epitome of the "anxious" art object, since the very ontological status of its image remains in question.

Among the important critical works on the *iconic* aspect of the photographic sign is Cindy Sherman's series of untitled studies for film stills. In these photographs, invariably "self-portraits," Sherman presents herself made up as an always different "heroine" of 1950s and 1960s Hollywood B-grade movies. While there exists a perfect congruence between author and image, there is an endless shift of persona presented by these portraits. Hence these are the hyperbolic instances of images as simulacra, where the person becomes nothing but a projected image of a stereotyped personality. Yet this conundrum on the structure of simulacral iconography is offered with an ironic twist; if the self is a fiction structured by the desire of the Other, and if the cinematic (Hollywood) image of woman is structured by male desire, then Sherman's images are the parody, or deconstruction, of such desire. Her images are the female representation of the object of male desire, in a totally narcissistic framework. Sherman opposes her own epistemophilia to male scoptophilia, in a significative system where the closure of reference (self-portraiture) is belied by the openness of the simulacral system (stereotypicality). The arbitrariness of the icon is revealed in a duplicitous presentation of true-author-as-false-idol. The images of women (of *a woman*) serve as a series of tropes, where authorship is made explicit while the subject is revealed as fictional. Mimesis creates icons, always false, but hardly less desirable for that deception. And, though these be stills from films never in fact produced, they nevertheless refer to an entire genre of films and an entire mode of desire still very much in vogue.

The *symbolic* aspect of the photographic sign is investigated in Barbara Kruger's works, for example her untitled 1984 photograph of a book open to a page on Impressionism, on which there rests a pair of eyeglasses distorting part of the text while framing the words, "my eye," and on which page are also collaged the words, "You are giving us the evil eye." The presence of linguistic text *as* photographic icon already achieves a disconcerting—anti-apotropaic—inmixing of different modes of signification, where it is impossible to determine whether image or text is the signifier or the signified, or even if they act together as one whole sign. And the confusion of text as metatext *and* as icon establishes an equivocation between epistemophilia and scoptophilia in the symbolic register. This situation is complicated by the use of the linguistic shifters "my," "you," and "us," which results in an ambiguous relation between image, author, photographer, and spectator/reader. The ambiguity of spectatorial/authorial position is even further complicated by an ambiguity in gender identification, contesting mainstream phallocentric subject construction in Western artistic imagery, thus attacking the core of the symbolic.

Yet however much we succeed in changing the object, however much we attempt to attack the symbolic, the photographic image will always consist of a subtle interplay of its iconic, symbolic, and indexical functions, just as the subject will always consist of the intertwining of the imaginary, symbolic, and real. All work on the object depends upon the formal structure of the signifier, and all criticism is but an explication of that structure, and of its sociological contextualization. In the postmodern realm, criticism differs from art in its sociological—and not semiological—function, now that photography has assumed the role of criticism.

Perhaps the most profound critical complication entailed by the postmodern condition is that it is no longer possible to determine unequivocally whether any given enunciation of image is a statement or a metastatement, while no enunciation (even, or especially, the metaphysical) may be deemed totally void of narrative content. This suggests a radical critique of the inherent Romantic expressionism of depth hermeneutics: signification is now realized as a *mise-en-abîme* of signifiers, where authorship and spectatorship are merely rhetorical/grammatical constructs; every signified is nothing but another signifier; literality is but another trope; depth a play of surfaces; the person is persona. A particularly complex example may delineate these differences.

In Toronto's Eaton Center (an ultra- or postmodernist enclosed shopping mall) is to be found Michael Snow's photographic sculpture *Flight Stop* (1979). This work consists of a flock of sixty fiberglass geese with applied black and white photographs, suspended from the mall's high ceiling, each formed in a different instance of flight posture. To examine the diffuse references of this work will disclose not only the very origins of modernism, but also the most contemporary simulacral productions of postmodernism.

(1) Most immediately, the presence of these geese—an emblem of Canada's vast wilderness, one of this country's remaining myths—within its most (post)modern architectural complex, surreptitiously creates the disquietude and ambiguity of the nature/culture distinction through the incongruity of the situation. Yet all the while this distinction is made manifest in the structure of the work itself, where the icon of a natural being is composed of artificial materials.

(2) The seemingly incongruous placement of this icon is perfectly coherent in relation to the iconography of Snow's previous photographic and cinematic works, in which the imagery of the Canadian wilderness is transformed into works of high modernism, a transformation exemplified by his now classic avant-garde film, *La région centrale* (in whose wilderness regions the geese would certainly not be out of place).

(3) Yet the particular form of the icons of *Flight Stop* are not exclusively Snow's. We find the earliest, and most direct, precedents of *Flight Stop* in the nineteenth-century stop-action sequential photographic experiments of Étienne Jules Marey and Eadweard Muybridge, works which were to give rise to

the cinema. Marey utilized his *chronophotography*—photographs composed of multiple exposures upon a single photographic plate—to study animal locomotion. In a work which serves as the formal origin of *Flight Stop*, Marey created three-dimensional models, derived from his photographs, of the positions of birds in flight. Thus the photographs which, according to common knowledge, were to give rise to the cinema first gave rise to sculpture. Interestingly enough, Muybridge's own protocinematic invention, the zoopraxiscope—comprised of a magic-lantern which projected painted images derived from Muybridge's photographs—was one in which the photographs that were also to give rise to cinema first gave rise to drawings. We might note the major difference between Marey's and Muybridge's techniques, since it entails critical aesthetic and metaphysical differences. Marey's works were composed of numerous shots of minimal time lapse (sixty images per second) on a single photographic plate; Muybridge's works were composed of numerous plates of stop-action shots, juxtaposed for sequential viewing. Needless to say, Muybridge's technique vastly increased the possibility of introducing narrative into the temporal sequence, all the while breaking up the continuity of the depicted motion (since the time lapse between images is more variable).[29] It is perhaps within the false scientificity and the cryptonarratology of this latter project that we may discover the narrative intent of Snow's minimalist artworks and effect our own entry into the narrative condition which we have termed postmodernism. The ambiguities and illusions which mark our experience of discrete visual differences are to be found both at the technical/optical origins of the cinema as well as the theoretical foundations of postmodernist artistic and theoretical production.

(4) The postmodern aspect of *Flight Stop* is revealed in its most literal, immediate aspect: its ultimately simulacral quality. More than a few of the viewers of this work believed the geese to be "real," stuffed geese (taxidermy as art), and there was even some conservationist outcry at their presence! The artwork, the artifice, is taken for a real object, to be denied both its representational status and its status as art. The artwork as

practical (and metaphysical) joke reveals the ridiculousness of critical and commonplace discourses, just as it evokes the sublimity of the wilderness to which it refers. Its very ontological status is evanescent, depending on the frame of reference: photograph as sculpture as protocinema as reality. Modernist by heritage; postmodernist by situation. Representational in its circular play of reference; simulacral in its illusionistic play of *trompe l'oeil.*

This work reaches back to the origins of photographic and cinematic practice, all the while projecting forward into the precession/procession of simulacra which governs our postmodern condition.[30] It reveals the complexity of the simulacral as well as the transformative possibilities of representation and may serve as an emblem of the articulation between modernism and postmodernism. As such, *Flight Stop* is a work which reveals the aporia that defines our existence, disclosing the major contemporary conditions of representability and simulacral production. These conditions, of course, are the forms of our consciousness.

9   broken voices, lost bodies: experimental radiophony

In the modern West, subjectivity has always been conceived of as a paradox, as a tension where interiority exists beneath the pressure of exteriority, and where technology exists as a metaphoric appendage of the body. One of the principal disjunctions or aporia guiding this study is between stream-of-consciousness (dream logic, depth psychology, libidinal primary processes, fantasy, interiorization) and stream-of-existence (aleatory constructs, the concrete, montage, cut-up, structuralization, exteriorization). The locus of nonsense reveals the limits, forms, and uses of rationality, as well as of the imaginary. Nonsense shall therefore be used as a testing mechanism, a transformative axis to fathom the limits, powers, and structures of sound, discourse, and art. Are we to make of nonsense nothing but a semiotic symptomatology of representation, and thus recuperate it within our rationality? Or shall it be appropriated in order to reveal the insidious role of media simulacra in contemporary life, and thus offer a *détournement* of such influences? Only continual mutation will offer a solution. Expression and communication shall be undermined by their own refusal; the spectacle will self-destruct, or it shall no longer be. This text will thus be a study of transmission, circuits, disarticulation, metamorphosis, mutation—and *not* communication, closure, articulation, representation, and simulacra.

Jacques Lacan, discussing the aesthetic implications of psychosis, accentuates "the lines of fragilization that define phantasmatic anatomy, manifested in the symptoms of schism (*schize*), spasm, or hysteria."[1] Might we not see in these "lines of fragilization" the very delineations of the *découpage, montage*, and *mixage* which are of concern to us? For just as the radio offers the possibility of creating new sounds, so too does it proffer the fantasy of a new, unthought of, unheard of body. We seek that realm where the voice reaches beyond its body, beyond the shadow of its corporeal origins, to become a radically original sonic object.

It is precisely in experimental and underground radio practice that such goals are most evidently instantiated. Consider Geert Lovink's description of contemporary underground radio in Amsterdam:

> They are not warming up samba, soul or schmaltz as the latest cult item or golden oldie for the purpose of playing on the collective memory, which so likes to be refreshed. They are not practicing audio history, trotting out near-extinct musical styles to get them interred in pop history. Material is collected and examined for its alienation potential. Trash is taken along on a trip, and treated with a certain respect, like a foreigner one passes the time with during travel. The processing is not an act of violence. It's not about ritually driving out some demon thought to reside in the media. The mix shows us that we must travel through an immense empty space before we arrive at a new meaning. Sovereign media, in their hard- as well as software, are hybrids through and through. Old and new, popular and obscure, trivial and heavy, everything is forged together into a stunning total mix. It is the mixmasters who connect discarded tape recorders to high-tech samplers and lace a cut-up Bush speech with a language course, barks and a dance orchestra.[2]

These radical experiments in radiophony provide an idea of the broad potential of radio beyond the various stultifying "laws" that guide mainstream radio: the law of maximal inoffensiveness, the law of maximal indifference, the law of maximal financial return. A sort of perverse specialization reigns in these contemporary pirate Amsterdam radio stations, which determine the margins of aesthetic culture. But there are also possibilities which operate at the very interior of mainstream, government, or commercial radio—parasites and viruses which determine yet other limits and other functions and pleasures of radiophony.

Every new medium first contains and disseminates the forms and content of past media, before ever revealing its own aesthetic potential. Radio was no exception, and present history has barely changed the situation. In his novel *Les larmes de pierre*, Eugène Nicole recounts a typical phantasm of the radio. The narrator, describing his childhood years on the island of Saint-Pierre in the 1940s, depicts the following:

> Maryse and I now know that the announcer didn't live in the radio. For a long time, at Jacquet's place, we imagined that the radio's interior was arranged like a miniature apartment where, at the same hour each evening, seated on a sofa, after having placed a record on the gramophone, Pointe-Fine spoke to us. . . . We readily admitted that *in the radio*—like in our dollhouses and our cardboard farms, which always had one wall missing, so that we could serve the childrens' refreshments, or put animals inside, stuck into the gaps by little wooden pegs—there reigned a different scale of peculiar realities. It was more difficult, however, to understand how that big asparagus Pointe-Fine, with his basque beret and his too-long raincoat, was to be found a half-hour later, not only in our radio, but in all the radios of the city. "The mystery of the Eucharist," exclaimed The Old Woman, raising her eyes to the heavens to underline our ignorance, or to ask pardon of God for this blasphemous parallel, which didn't hinder her from adding, "Like the body of Jesus, while present in each host, is in all the others at the same time."[3]

In The *Uses of Enchantment,* the psychoanalyst Bruno Bettelheim explains that illustrated versions of fairy tales should not be read to children, as the images encroach upon and hinder the psychological projections of the children's individual fantasies and desires. The principle behind this precept also specifies the position and potential of radiophony in the *imaginaire.* What is at stake is not merely the imagination as rememoration, as the reproduction what already exists, but rather the imagination as a creative act. Radio is the ideal medium to establish such a poetics and ethics, given its infinite overture to imaginative conjecture and visual discord. Yet seldom is such aesthetic openness manifested or even encouraged in modern media; mainstream radio ironically uses all of its efforts to deny this poetic source of creativity, by restricting radio to old musical and theatrical conventions, by remaining a "clean" medium.

However sophisticated the montage, most works for radio never surpass the conditions of music, theater, poetry—radio rarely realizes its truly radiophonic potentials. For radiophony is not only a matter of audiophonic invention, but also of sound diffusion and listener circuits or feedback. Whence the paradox of radio: a universally public transmission is heard in the most private of circumstances; the thematic specificity of each individual broadcast, its imaginary scenario, is heard within an infinitely diverse set of nonspecific situations, different for each listener; the radio's putative shared solidarity of auditors in fact achieves their atomization, as well as a reification of the imagination. The Old Woman is correct: the experience of radio is indeed mystifying, though on a far more mundane level than her analogy would suggest.

In contrast with Eugène Nicole's charming childhood fantasy of radio, consider the following description by the contemporary radio artist, Gregory Whitehead:

> Radio Talking Drum—an utopian transposition that loves to forget. *Most* forgotten are the lethal wires that still heat up from inside out, wires that connect radio with warfare, brain damage, rattles from necropolis. When I turn my radio on, I hear a whole chorus of death rattles: from stone cold, hard fact larynxes frozen at every stage of physical decomposition; from talk show golden throats cut with a scalpel, transected, then taped back together and beamed out across the airwaves; from voices that have been severed from the body for so long that no one can remember who they belong to, or whether they belong to anybody at all; from pop monster giggle-bodies guaranteed to shake yo' booty; from artificial folds sneak-stitched into still-living throats through computer synthesis and digital processing; from mechanical chatter-boxes dead to begin with; from cyberphonic anti-bodies taking flight and crashing to pieces on air.[4]

The human-in-the-radio is countered by the radio-in-the-human. Like Nicole, Whitehead recognizes radio's intimate coupling with sundry nostalgias and forms of death—radio as an electronic *memento mori* for a modern age and a thoughtless public.

Sound recording was originally invented to preserve voices beyond the grave in a sort of frozen speech; radio would establish the dissemination of those very same voices.[5] The phantasms behind the origins of sound recording were not very different. Edison patented the phonograph in 1877, the same year that Charles Cros invented a similar device in France. Edison's initial motivation was to preserve, and not replicate or transmit, sound. More specifically, he wrote that "We will be able to preserve and hear again, one year or one century later, a memorable speech, a worthy tribune, a famous singer, etc. . . . We could use it in a more private manner: to preserve religiously the last words of a dying man, the voice of one who has died, of a distant parent, a lover, a mistress."[6] Sound fidelity was to help heal the wounds of nostalgia and to prolong the more fickle emotional fidelity of love—signified in the very timbre of the human voice and now made available to an ever-fading memory. Where once total silence was only possible in death, now the dead continue to speak, sing, make noise, and pollute the body politic, leading to an eerie epistemological rupture.

Regarding the shift from music composed in the epoch of a representational episteme to twentieth-century music conditioned by electromechanical repetition and proliferation, Jacques Attali explains that: "Crisis is no longer a breakdown, a rupture, as in representation, but a decrease in the efficiency of the production of demand, an excess of repetition. *Metaphorically, it is like cancer, while the crisis of representation is like cardiac arrest.*"[7] In this simulacral economy, sounds circulate without origin or end, while the age-old metaphorization of the ideal body vanishes in an allegory of pathological mutations. Whitehead's Forensic Theater provides an analytic of this electropathology. Radiophonic airspace is a necropolis riddled with dead voices, the voices of the dead, and dead air—all cut off from their originary bodies, all now transmitted to the outer international and cosmic airwaves only in order to reenter our inner ears in a "mad *Totentanz*."[8] Whence the need to establish a hermeneutic model based on the morbid anatomy of postmortem vocal activity. The "schizophonic" condition of the recorded and broadcast voice is that of the separation of the acoustic event from the lived, eroticized, speaking body. This permits the subsequent dispersal of the disembodied utterance—circulating and decaying on the airwaves, existing beyond the death of the speaking subject. Thanks to recording, our speech has an afterlife, fated to transformation, decay, loss, misprision. Or, as radio producer-theoretician Christof Migone explains, "The static that populates radio air implies a variety of (mis)understandings," irrevocably leading to the recognition that "The disarticulation of the original is not to be regarded as sacrilege, but certainly as transgression. The triad—transmission/translation/transgression—shares more than a prefix, it implies a common phenomenology: radio."[9] Radiophony is guided by the serendipity of a *fata morgana*, the bewildering, aleatory process of recuperating and rechanneling the lost voice.

Such is the *principia schizophonica*. In radiophony, not only is the voice separated from the body, and not only does it return to the speaker as a disembodied presence, it is furthermore thrust into the public arena to mix its sonic destiny with that of other voices. Whitehead defines the ontological structure of radio as, "a public channel produced by an absent other entering into a private ear. The material specific to radio inscribes itself within the thoroughly unpredictable libidinal circulations internal to a ménage-à-trois. The language of radio is thus constructed not from a series of applied techniques, but from a series of fragile complicities."[10] The ontological status of this sound object is what Michel Chion writes of as the *acousmetric*, referring to a system where sound appears without any corresponding visual correlate—the very feature which permits the radio to be experienced as a spiritual or paranoid receiver, as well as an artistic muse.[11] Whitehead: "From dissemination, a transmission; from transmission, an interference; from interference, a complicity; and from complicity, the sound of something dripping in the darkest caverns of the cerebral cave."[12] As is the case of Artaud, Wölfli, and Wolfson, the range of inner sounds is as broad as the cosmos, as complex as language, as dense as the viscera, and totally unpredictable. Consider Alberto Savinio's short story "Psyche," where the protagonist writes of one character: "Charles Magne had an uncle in Salonika, a piano tuner and the proprietor of a music shop on Egnazia Street. Charles Magne's uncle was a schizophrenic, and when he was taken to the mental hospital he brandished his tuning fork and shouted out that he wanted to tune the vocal chords of all humanity."[13] As opposed to the benevolence of Savinio's melomaniacal personnage, Whitehead's schizophonic would, quite to the contrary, wish to set all of our voices out of tune, indeed out of body, in a psycho-acoustic meltdown or mix-up. It is precisely at the radical limits of radiophony, in its extreme differentiation from the theatrical, musical, poetic, and audio arts, that we can situate the aesthetic practice of Gregory Whitehead—simultaneously a hermeneutic of the morbid disembodied voice and a poetics of schizophonically deteriorating enunciation. Such is a new body politic supported by the prosthetic language of the disembody, the antibody, the nobody, the radiobody.[14] In such work, not only will the radiophonic medium be contaminated by disarticulated voices, but in turn the voice, our own voices, will be infected by the prosthetic capabilities and shock tactics of the electronic media.[15]

In August 1989 the Austrialian Broadcasting Company (ABC) program called "The Listening Room" aired a documentary produced by Virginia Madsen entitled *Taken by Speed*, dealing with the relations between speed and technology as analyzed in the writings of Paul Virilio. Virilio insists that war requires a logic of accidents, a wisdom derived from the absolute expression of technological risk. In an apparent reversal of Aristotelian logic, he explains that this wisdom is a function of the symmetry between substance and accident. Catastrophe theory becomes not a matter of ruins and effect, but of cinematic and dynamic processes, an exploration of degeneration, decomposition, disintegration, disappearance.[16]

At one point in this radio broadcast, the awe of technology is revealed by children's voices as they explore a hypothetical Museum of Accidents, described as follows:

> Founded 1992. As decreed by the people to have its aim to collect, categorise, define, and to display to the citizens all accidents, disasters, aberrations, mutations, meltdowns, power failures, computer shutdowns, viruses, severed limbs, artificial organs, skipped beats, slipped discs, slips of the tongue, sleights of hand, sunken continents, sunken ships, lost libraries, lost tongues, wreckages of machines, databanks, electronic wiring, accidental discoveries, redundancies, archaisms, space junk, hunks of meteors and asteroids, science fiction writers.[17]

This imaginary musteum—displaying an iconology of technofailure à la J. G. Ballard—could serve (in its sonic manifestations) as a prolegomenon to a work also produced by the ABC the year after, Gregory Whitehead's *Pressures of the Unspeakable:* "In addition to framing the nervous system, the *telephone-microphone-tape-recorder-radio* circuitry also provided the key for the acoustic demarcation of *pressure in the system*: distortion, the disruption of digital codes, pure unmanageable noise. The scream as an eruption in excess of prescribed circuitries, as capable of 'blowing' communications technologies not designed for such extreme and unspeakable meanings."[18] He produced the "screamscape" of Sydney.

What is certain is that this "nervous system" is simultaneously that of Sydney *and* of Whitehead *and* of radio circuitry—all of which coalesce into a possible alter ego for the moments of our most severe nervous tension. Whitehead substantiates the epistemological conditions of this nearly unendurable "system" with a citation from Wittgenstein: "When you are philosophising, you must descend into primeval chaos and feel at home there."[19] For the scream reveals the chaotic depths of linguistic and vocal systems. We may complicate these considerations even further, siding with Artaud and Bataille and parodying Wittgenstein, in claiming that "What cannot be said must result in the outburst of a scream."

notes

Introduction

1. Kaja Silverman, "Lost Objects and Mistaken Subjects: Film Theory's Structuring Lack," *Wide Angle* 7, nos. 1 and 2 (1985): 14.

2. Laura Mulvey, "Visual Pleasure and Narrative Cinema," *Screen* 16, no. 3 (1975): 8–18.

3. Paul de Man, *The Resistance to Theory* (Minneapolis: Univ. of Minnesota Press, 1986).

4. Quoted in Gustav Janouch, *Conversations with Kafka* (New York: New Directions, 1971), p. 152.

5. See Sigmund Freud, "Fetishism" (1927), in *Sexuality and the Psychology of Love* (New York: Collier, 1963), pp. 214–19.

6. Georges Bataille, "L'esprit moderne et le jeu des transpositions," in *Oeuvres Complètes,* vol. 1 (Paris: Gallimard, 1970), p. 273.

7. See Christian Metz, *Le signifiant imaginaire* (Paris: Union Générale d'Editions, 1977).

8. Roland Barthes, "Les sorties du texte," in *Le bruissement de la langue* (Paris: Seuil, 1984), p. 273.

9. Mulvey, "Visual Pleasure," p. 18.

10. Marcel Proust, *Le temps retrouvé* (Paris: Flammarion, 1986), pp. 276–77.

11. Jorge Luis Borges, "Tlön, Uqbar, Orbis Tertius," in *Labyrinths,* trans. Donald A. Yates and James E. Irby (New York: New Directions, 1964), p. 10.

12. My tales from a forthcoming book, *The Aphoristic Theater,* explore the intersecting domains of theory and fiction. See my "Baudelaire's Demons" and "Nietzsche's Epiphany," in *Public* 7 (Toronto, 1993): *Sacred Technologies*; pp. 89–93 and 171–73.

Chapter 1. Iconology and Perversion

1. "The epitrope, in view of turning us away from an excess, striking us with its horror, or making us repent of it, in fact seems to invite us to give ourselves over to it without reserve, through an ultimate provocation, beyond all measure." This somewhat archaic definition of an equally archaic trope is from Pierre Fontanier, *Les Figures du discours* (Paris, Flammarion, 1977); originally published in 1830.

2. Cited in Pierre Maraval, "Epiphane, 'Docteur des iconoclastes,' " in *Nicée II, 787–1987: Douze siècles d'images religieuses,* ed. F. Boespflug and N. Lossky (Paris: Editions du Cerf, 1987), p. 59. I am deeply indebted to this excellent collection of essays on the iconoclastic controversy for much of the information and several of the anecdotes which I present here on this topic. For another account of contemporary iconoclasm in relation to the tradition, see Juan Davila and Paul Foss, *The Mutilated Pieta,* Art & Criticism Monograph Series, vol. 1 (Melbourne: Artspace, 1985).

3. Sigmund Freud, *The Ego and the Id,* trans. Joan Riviere (New York: Norton, 1962), p. 16.

4. Maurice Merleau-Ponty, *Phenomenology of Perception,* trans. Colin Smith (London: Routledge & Kegan Paul, 1970), p. 237.

5. Michel Foucault, "Nietzsche, Genealogy, History," in *Language, Counter-Memory, Practice,* trans. Donald F. Bouchard and Sherry Simon (Ithaca: Cornell Univ. Press, 1977). p. 148.

6. Jean-François Lyotard, *Economie libidinale* (Paris: Minuit, 1974), p. 26.

7. Friedrich Nietzsche, *On the Genealogy of Morals* (1887), trans. Walter Kaufmann (New York: Random House, 1969), p. 61.

8. Gilles Deleuze and Félix Guattari, *Anti-Oedipus: Capitalism and Schizophrenia,* trans. Robert Hurley, Mark Seem, and Helen R. Lane (New York: Viking, 1977), p. 190.

9. Pierre Clastres, *La société contre l'état* (Paris: Minuit, 1974).

10. We should not be at all surprised at the extreme popularity of an exhibit of medieval torture devices which traveled through Europe on exhibition from 1983 to 1987. We should note that though modern methods of torture are often more insidious, many of them were developed precisely in order to leave no trace upon the body, in order to avoid possible juridical complications.

11. We might note that one of the principal social functions of the second Nicene Council was the reintegration of the iconoclastic bishops into the orthodox Christian community. The preconditions for this reintegration were the confession of belief in the intercession of the Virgin and the saints, the acceptance of saintly relics, and the gestures of prostration before, and kissing of, the relics and icons of Christ, the Virgin, and the saints. The iconoclasts had to show signs of iconophilia, which extended to the representations of the human—and not only divine—body. The veneration of icons permitted a great extension of the cult of the saints and the Virgin which, at times, came into direct conflict with church dogma, since such cults often circumvented the powers of the priesthood and counteracted the powers of God, powers which the inauguration of icons was initially intended to accentuate and support.

12. Cited in *Nicée II,* ed. Boespflug and Lossky, p. 133.

13. Roland Barthes, *A Lover's Discourse,* trans. Richard Howard (New York: Hill & Wang, 1978). The resolution of the iconoclastic controversy established the theological foundations of the problem of the incarnation—i.e., the relations between Christ's human and divine natures—and the special issue of its representation and iconology. Cf. Constantin Scouteris, "La personne du verbe incarné et i'icône," in

Nicée II, ed. Boespflug and Lossky, pp. 121–33. The psychological structure of fetishism is also founded on the relations between the visible and invisible (phallus). For an excellent discussion of this topic, see Guy Rosolato, "Etude des perversions sexuelles à partir du fétishisme," in *Le désir et la perversion* (Paris: Seuil, 1967), pp. 9–52. Rosolato shows the striking parallels between the psychological structure of fetishism and Gnostic theology, especially in regard to their revolutionary, transgressive position vis-à-vis the symbolic law. Unfortunately, a discussion of this theme is beyond the scope of this essay. But see Paul Foss, "Eyes, Fetishism, and the Gaze," *Art & Text* 20 (1986): 24–41.

14. Georges Bataille, "Sacrifices," in *Oeuvres complètes,* vol. 1 (Paris: Gallimard, 1970), p. 94.

15. Cf. Guy Rosolato, "L'oscillation métaphoro-métonymique," in *La relation d'inconnu* (Paris: Gallimard, 1978), pp. 52–80.

16. Rosolato, "Que contemplait Freud sur 'Acropole'?" in *La relation d'inconnu,* p. 249.

17. The iconic form has no a priori sacred character (unlike the relic, which is directly related to a sacred person). On the one hand, any particular beautiful female image may be designated as either "Mary" or as "Venus"; on the other hand, the particular details of the representation of the Virgin are only partially coded and determined. There is a vast zone of "free play" in which the artist's own style may be manifested, and even occasionally circumvent and subvert the conventional meaning of the depicted scenario. Note that the Roman Catholic iconographic tradition is considerably more flexible than the rather rigid and highly codified Byzantine tradition. [The role of marginalia and incidental details within Christian iconography is thoroughly investigated in the works of Jurgis Baltrušaitis, notably *Formations, déformations: La stylistique ornementale dans la sculpture romaine* (Paris: Flammarion, 1986; originally published in 1931); *Le Moyen Age fantastique: Antiquités et exotismes dans l'art gothique* (Paris: Flammarion, 1981; originally published in 1955); and *Réveils et prodiges: le gothique fantastique* (1960). These works not only teach us the (usually hidden) meaning of "pure" ornament, but also show how such ornamentation must force us to rethink traditional iconology.]

18. Yukio Mishima, *Confessions of a Mask* (1949), trans. Meredith Weatherby (New York: New Directions, 1958), pp. 37–47.

19. Mishima, *Sun and Steel* (1968), trans. John Bester (New York: Grove Press, 1970), p. 7.

20. Cf. Allen S. Weiss, "Ideology and the Problem of Style: The Errant Text," *Enclitic* 14 (1983): 17–23. On the delirious transformation of commonplace objects into cosmic symbols, consider Witold Gombrowicz, *Cosmos* (1965); Italo Calvino, *Mr. Palomar* (1983); Jorge Luis Borges, *The God's Script* (c. 1949).

21. Nietzsche, *Thus Spoke Zarathustra* (1883–85), ed. Walter Kaufmann, *The Portable Nietzsche* (New York: Penguin, 1968). p. 146.

22. Gaston Bachelard, *Lautréamont* (Paris: José Corti, 1939), pp. 103–15.

23. Bataille, "Sacrifices," p. 91.

24. Marcel Proust, *Du côté de chez Swann* (Paris: Gallimard, 1954; originally published in 1913), p. 13.

25. Harold Bloom, "Freud and the Sublime," in *Agon: Towards a Theory of Revisionism* (New York: Oxford Univ. Press, 1982), pp. 108–9. Bloom's notion of "misreading" is central to our concern.

26. Kurt Eissler, *Leonardo da Vinci,* cited in Jean Laplanche, *La sublimation* (Paris: Presses Universitaires de France, 1980), p. 231.

27. Bataille, "Informe," in *Oeuvres complètes,* vol. 1, p. 217.

28. Leonardo da Vinci, *Notebooks,* vol. 2, ed. Jean Paul Richter (New York: Dover, 1970), p. 129.

29. Leonardo himself remarks on the formal relations between curls of hair and the motion of swirling water *(Notebooks,* vol. 1, p. 200). On the many forms and functions of water in the poetic imagination, see Gaston Bachelard, *L'Eau et les rêves* (Paris: José Corti, 1942); for a psychoanalytical theory of the symbolic function of water in relation to Eros and Thanatos, see Sandor Ferenczi, *Thalassa: A Theory of Genitality* (1923), trans. Henry Alden Bunker (New York, Norton, 1968).

30. Bataille, "Madame Edwarda," *Oeuvres complètes,* vol. 3, pp. 20–21.

31. Maurice Rheims, *La vie secrète des objets* (Paris: 10/18, 1963). p. 47.

Chapter 3. Innate Totems

1. Antonin Artaud, "Manifeste en langage clair" (1925), in *Oeuvres complètes* vol. 3 (Paris: Gallimard), p. 52; citations from the *Complete Works* are hereafter cited in the text by volume and page number(s).

2. From Artaud's notebooks of February 1947, cited in *Antonin Artaud: Dessins,* ed. Paule Thévenin (Paris: Centre Georges Pompidou, 1987), p. 18.

3. Artaud, *Nouveaux écrits de Rodez,* p. 82.

4. Antonin Artaud, "Le visage humain . . . ," text in *Portraits et dessins par Antonin Artaud,* the exhibition catalogue of his drawings at the Galerie Pierre, Paris, 4–20 July 1947. Cited in *Antonin Artaud: Dessins,* ed. Thévenin, p. 50.

5. Ibid., p. 50.

6. Cited in *Antonin Artaud: Dessins et portraits,* ed. Paule Thévenin and Jacques Derrida (Paris: Gallimard, 1986), p. 26.

7. T. S. Eliot, "The Hollow Men" (1925), in *T. S. Eliot: The Complete Poetry and Plays 1909–1950* (New York: Harcourt, Brace & World, 1971), pp. 58–59.

8. Jacques Lacan, "Le stade du miroir comme formateur de la fonction du je," in *Écrits 1* (Paris: Seuil, 1966), p. 94.

9. *Artaud: Dessins et portraits,* ed. Thévenin and Derrida, p. 81.

Chapter 4. Pressures of the Sun

1. All Antonin Artaud, *Oeuvres complètes,* vol. 9 (Paris: Gallimard, 1956–present), p. 37; all subsequent citations appear parenthetically in the text.

Chapter 5. Between the Desire and the Spasm

1. See my "A New History of the Passions," in *The Aesthetics of Excess* (Albany: SUNY Press, 1989), p. 43–53.

2. Lettrist International Collective, "Réponse à une enquête du groupe surréaliste belge," *Potlach* 5 (1954), republished in *Potlach* (Paris: Editions Gérard Lebovici, 1985), p. 38.

3. Guy Debord, *La Société du spectacle* (Paris: Editions Gérard Lebovici, 1987, orig. pub. 1967), p. 10.

4. Ibid., p. 22

5. See the anonymously written "Problèmes préliminaires à la construction d'une situation," *Internationale Situationniste* 1 (1958) [rpt. Editions Gérard Lebovici, 1975]): 11.

6. Debord, "Thèses sur la révolution culturelle," *Internationale Situationniste* 1 (1958): 21.

7. Maurice Merleau-Ponty, "Eye and Mind" [1961], in *The Primacy of Perception,* trans. Carleton Dallery (Evanston: Northwestern Univ. Press, 1964), p. 162.

8. Merleau-Ponty, *Phenomenology of Perception* [1945], trans. Colin Smith (London: Routledge & Kegan Paul, 1970), p. 237.

9. Ibid., p. 237. See my "Merleau-Ponty's Concept of the 'Flesh' as Libido Theory," *Substance* 30 (1981): 85–95.

10. Merleau-Ponty, *The Visible and the Invisible* [1964], trans. Alphonso Lingis (Evanston: Northwestern Univ. Press, 1968), p. 270.

11. "Eye and Mind," p. 166.

12. *Visible and the Invisible,* p. 184.

13. Jean-François Lyotard, "Sur une figure de discours," in *Des dispositifs pulsionnels* (Paris: U.G.E. [10/18], 1973), p. 140.

14. Lyotard, *Discours, figure* (Paris: Klincksieck, 1971), p. 328.

15. Lyotard, *Economie libidinale* (Paris: Minuit, 1974), p. 9ff.

16. Lyotard, "La Peinture comme dispositif libidinal" (1972), in *Des dispositifs pulsionnels,* p. 239.

17. Lyotard, *Dispositifs,* p. 248. See also his *Les transformateurs Duchamp* (Paris: Galilée, 1977).

18. *Discours, figure*, p. 279.

19. See Vincent Descombes, *Le Même et l'autre* (Paris: Minuit, 1979), p. 179.

20. Gilles Deleuze and Félix Guattari, *Anti-Oedipus: Capitalism and Schizophrenia* (1972), trans. Robert Hurley, Mark Seem, Helen R. Lane (New York: Viking Press, 1977), p. 30 and passim.

21. *Anti-Oedipe,* p. 39.

22. *Anti-Oedipe,* p. 31.

23. Deleuze, *Francis Bacon: Logique de la sensation* (Paris: Editions de la différence, 1981), p. 16.

24. *Francis Bacon,* p. 41.

25. "Eye and Mind," p. 83; 99ff.

26. See the acts of the colloquium at Cerisy, published as *Artaud* (Paris: U.G.E. [10/18], 1973).

27. *Anti-Oedipe,* p. 19.

28. *OC*, 13: 104. Translation by Clayton Eshleman and Norman Glass, in *Antonin Artaud: Four Texts* (Los Angeles: Panjandrum Books, 1982), p. 79. See my "Radiophonic Art: The Voice of the Impossible Body," *Discourse*, 14, no. 2 (1992); and "Radio, Death and the Devil: On Artaud's *Pour en finir avec le jugement de Dieu,* in *Wireless Imagination,* ed. Douglas Kahn and Gregory Whitehead (Cambridge, Mass: M.I.T. Press, 1992).

29. Marcel Duchamp, "The Creative Act (1957), in *the Essential Writings of Marcel Duchamp,* ed. Michel Sanouillet and Elmer Paterson (London: Thames & Hudson, 1975), pp. 138–40.

30. Harald Szeeman, ed., *Junggesellenmaschinen/Les Machines célibataires* (Venice: Alfieri, 1975).

31. Guy Rosolato, "Étude des perversions sexuelles à partir du fétichisme," in *Le Désir et la perversion* (Paris: Seuil, 1967), pp. 9–52. See also his *Essais sur le symbolique* (Paris: Gallimard, 1964); *La Relation d'inconnu* (Paris: Gallimard, 1978); and *Eléments de l'interprétation* (Paris: Gallimard, 1985).

Chapter 6. Formations of Subjectivity and Sexual Identity

1. See Annette Michelson, " 'Anémic cinéma': Reflections on an Emblematic Work," *Artforum* 12, no. 2 (1973): 64–69. This work also contains a discussion of Duchamp's *Tu m'* (see below). On the erotic implications of the texts in *Anémic cinéma,* see P. Adams Sitney, "Image and Title in Avant-Garde Cinema," *October* 11 (1979): 97–112.

2. On the relationship between the disruption and consequent reorganization of discrete phonetic entities, see Allen S. Weiss, "The Other as Muse: On the Ontology and Aesthetics of Narcissism," in *Psychosis and Sexual Identity: Toward a Post-Analytic View of the Schreber Case,* ed. David B. Allison, Prado de Oliveira, Mark S. Roberts, Allen S. Weiss (Albany: State Univ. of New York Press, 1988), pp. 70–87.

3. Marcel Duchamp, "The Green Box," in *The Essential Writings of Marcel Duchamp,* ed. Michel Sanouillet and Elmer Peterson (London: Thames and Hudson, 1975), p. 30.

4. Ibid., p. 107. Note a similar "transsexualism" or transvestism in Duchamp's *L.H.O.O.Q.,* where the Mona Lisa appears with moustache and goatee. Duchamp's work abounds in such sexual inversions.

5. Ibid., p. 30.

6. Ibid., p. 140.

7. Janine Chasseguet-Smirgel, "On President Schreber's Transsexual Delusion," in *Psychosis and Sexual Identity,* pp. 155–68.

8. Sarah Kofman, *L'enfance de l'art* (Paris: Payot, 1970), pp. 163–74.

9. Chasseguet-Smirgel, "On President Schreber's Transsexual Delusion."

10. On the role of titles in Surrealist cinema, see Sitney, "Image and Title."

11. *Webster's Third New International Dictionary,* vol. 2 (Chicago: G. & C. Merriam Co., 1966), s.v. "I."

12. Jean-François Lyotard, *Les transformateurs Duchamp* (Paris: Galilée, 1977), p. 101.

13. Hollis Frampton, "Letters from Framp," *October* 32 (1985): 38–39. This is a special issue of *October* on Frampton.

14. For example, consider Frampton's films: *Palindrome* (1969), which is precisely what its title indicates; the interpolation of graphic texts within the photographic shots of scenes in depth in *More Than Meets the Eye* (1979); the cinematic pun on Duchamp's *La mariée mise à nu par ses célibataires, même,* where an archaic film depicting one man distracting a young woman while a second man unravels her dress by pulling on a thread is used in Frampton's film *Cadenza I* (1977–80); also see his photographic work *Tomatoes Descending a Ramp,* an obvious reference to Duchamp's *Nude Descending a Staircase;* Frampton's photographic portrait of Larry Poons (1963) reveals in the background two shadows of hatracks, recalling Duchamp's 1917 readymade *Hat Rack,* the shadow of which appeared as an iconographic feature of his later *Tu m'* (1918).

15. See Annette Michelson, "Frampton's Sieve," *October* 32 (1985): 151–66; and Allen S. Weiss, "Cartesian Simulacra," *Persistence of Vision* 5 (1987): 55–61. *Poetic Justice* also appeared in book form (Rochester: Visual Studies Workshop Press, 1973).

16. Emile Benveniste, "La nature des pronoms," in *Problèmes de linguistique générale,* vol. 1 (Paris: Gallimard, 1966), pp. 251–70.

17. Roman Jakobson, "Les embrayeurs, les catégories verbales et le verbe russe," in *Essais de linguistique générale* (Paris: Minuit, 1963), p. 179.

18. Emile Benveniste, "De la subjectivité dans le langage," in *Problèmes de linguistique générale,* pp. 257–66.

19. Julia Kristeva, *La révolution du langage poétique* (Paris: Seuil, 1974), pp. 324–35; see also Kristeva's "The Speaking Subject," in *On Signs,* ed. Marshall Blonsky (Baltimore: Johns Hopkins Univ. Press, 1985), pp. 210–20.

20. Benveniste, "De la subjectivité dans le langage," p. 260.

21. Anthony Wilden, *The Language of the Self* (New York: Dell, 1968), p. 219.

22. Emmanuel Levinas, *Totality and Infinity,* trans. Alphonso Lingis (Pittsburgh: Duquesne Univ. Press, 1969). For a useful introduction to current research on Levinas, especially his model of eroticism, see Elizabeth Grosz, "The 'People of the Book': Representation and Alterity in Emmanuel Levinas," *Art & Text* 26 (1987): 32–40; see also the important collection of critical essays, *Face to Face with Levinas,* ed. Richard Cohen (Albany: State Univ. of New York Press, 1986).

23. Levinas, *Totality and Infinity,* p. 195.

24. Ibid., p. 262.

25. Emmanuel Levinas, "On the Trail of the Other," *Philosophy Today* 10, no. 1 (1966): 42. (Note that the translation of the title contains a serious metaphysical error: it should be "The Trace of the Other.")

26. An influential statement on this problem is Laura Mulvey, "Visual Pleasure and Narrative Cinema," *Screen* 16, no. 3 (1975): 6–18. For a rather different approach to the problems of fetishism, fascination, and identification in the cinema, see Allen S. Weiss, "An Eye for an I: On the Art of Fascination," *SubStance* 51 (1986): 87–95. Needless to say, the problematic of identification is far more complex than the present article indicates: the intersections of this notion in psychoanalytic theory, libido theory, and structural linguistics will be attempted in a future work. Whether or not identificatory patterns in "mainstream" and "avant-garde" cinema can be dealt with according to the same principles is also a crucial topic of study.

27. Luce Irigaray, "Communications linguistique et spéculaire," in *Parler n'est jamais neutre* (Paris: Minuit, 1985), pp. 15–34.

28. Kristeva, "The Speaking Subject," p. 219. The apparent essentialism of Kristeva's analysis, especially in regard to her understanding of the privileged position of the maternal body in the imaginary, has been criticized by certain feminist writers. But, since for her the ultimate psychogenetic constitution of subjectivity is a function of discourse—a symbolic function—it would seem that in fact this model of subject constitution would be antiessentialist. For an excellent study of this problematic, see Mary Ann Doane, "Woman's Stake: Filming the Female Body," *October* 17 (1981): 23–26. It is true, as Doane claims, that the essentialist/antiessentialist difference in the feminist debate must be overcome. We might ask if Kristeva's vacillation between these two positions is simply a matter of inconsistency, or rather if we find there—at the intersection of libidinal economies and symbolic formations— a solution to this problem.

29. Michelson, "Frampton's Sieve," p. 166.

30. Benveniste, "La nature des pronoms," p. 251.

31. This problematic was investigated in a seminar on Heideggerian phenomenology at SUNY Stony Brook in 1975, organized by Don Ihde. In the broadest ontological sense, Hegelian phenomenology instantiates the disembodied description of subject position, while Levinas's phenomenology instantiates the embodied position.

32. Anna Freud, *The Ego and the Mechanisms of Defense* (New York: International Universities Press, 1966), p. 103.

33. The problematic of active and reactive modes of consciousness finds its locus classicus in Nietzsche's *On the Genealogy of Morals;* the major systematic development of this issue is in Gilles Deleuze, *Nietzsche et la philosophie* (Paris: Presses Universitaires de France, 1973). The difference between reaction formation and sublimated repetition of pleasure is equivalent to the difference between repetition in the Hegelian dialectic and the Nietzschean affirmation of the Eternal Return, *mutatis mutandis.*

34. Harold Bloom, "Freud's Concepts of Defense and the Poetic Will," in *Agon: Towards a Theory of Revisionism* (New York: Oxford Univ. Press, 1982), p. 139.

35. Harold Bloom, *The Anxiety of Influence* (New York: Oxford Univ. Press, 1973), p. 95.

36. Hollis Frampton, "Notes on Composing in Film," in *Circles of Confusion* (Rochester: Visual Studies Workshop Press, 1983), p. 119.

37. Ibid., p. 121.

38. Freud, *Ego and the Mechanisms of Defense*, p. 91.

39. Christopher Phillips, "Word Pictures: Frampton and Photography," *October* 32 (1985): 69.

40. Frampton, "Eadweard Muybridge: Fragments of a Tesseract," in *Circles of Confusion*, p. 75.

41. Frampton, "Impromptus on Edward Weston: Everything in its Place," in *Circles of Confusion*, p. 148.

42. Harold Bloom, "Freud's Concept of Defense and the Poetic Will," p. 124.

43. Frampton, "Incisions in History/Fragments of Eternity," in *Circles of Confusion*, p. 101.

44. Frampton, "Impromptus on Edward Weston," p. 151.

45. Ibid., p. 149

46. Ibid., p. 147, emphasis added.

47. Hollis Frampton, "For a Metahistory of Film: Commonplace Notes and Hypotheses," in *Circles of Confusion*, p. 111. On the role of brief shots based on still photography in Frampton's films, see Allen S. Weiss, "Frampton's Lemma, Zorn's Dilemma," *October* 32 (1985): 118–28. We might note that Frampton in fact attempted to use still photographs in *Zorns Lemma* (1970), but this resulted in too static a film: he had to *film* the very same scenes. Thus he finally failed to incorporate still photography in this film. It was rather in *nostalgia* (1971) that Frampton provided an extended study of film, photography, and the temporality of memory.

48. Frampton, "Impromptus on Edward Weston," p. 151. We might note that the reactions to Weston's photography (for example, the famous shots of the chambered nautilus shells of 1927) emphasize the eroticism of these works. See *Edward Weston* (New York: Aperture, 1965), pp. 21–22.

49. Frampton, "Impromptus on Edward Weston," p. 148.

Chapter 7. Acting, Identity, and Scenarization

1. Sigmund Freud, "A Case of Paranoia Running Counter to the Psychoanalytical Theory of the Disease," in *Sexuality and the Psychology of Love* (New York: Collier, 1963), p. 97. Consult Freud's text for the details of this case study. The disclaimer of the suppression of characteristic details is made throughout his writings, as for example in "The Psychogenesis of a Case of Homosexuality in a Woman," in the same volume.

2. Plato, *The Republic*, book 10; on the relations between the particular and the universal in aesthetic theory, see Allen S. Weiss, "Ideology and the Problem of Style: The Errant Text," *Enclitic* 14 (1983), republished in Allen S. Weiss, *The Aesthetics of Excess* (Albany: State Univ. of New York Press, 1989).

3. See the classic text on phantasms, J. Laplanche and J.-B. Pontalis, "Fantasme originaire, fantasmes des origines, origine du fantasme." *Les Temps Modernes* 215, pp. 1833–68. For an account of the aesthetic implications of phantasmatic organisation, see Allen S. Weiss, "A Logic of the Simulacrum, or the Anti-Roberte," *Art & Text* 18 (1985), reprinted in *The Aesthetics of Excess*.

4. Guy Rosolato, "Paranoia et scène primitive," in *Essais sur le symbolique* (Paris: Gallimard, 1969), p. 205.

5. Laplanche and Pontalis, "Fantasme originaire, fantasmes des origines, origine du fantasme," p. 1868.

6. Ibid., p. 1853.

7. Ibid., p. 1850.

8. Rosolato, "Paranoia et scène primitive," p. 202.

9. Ibid., pp. 217*ff*; for Freud's original account of this combinatory identificatory apparatus, see "On the Mechanism of Paranoia," in *General Psychological Theory* (New York: Collier, 1970).

10. On the dreamwork, see Freud, *The Interpretation of Dreams,* part 4. We might note, as a famous and revealing literary example of multiple identifications of the self in a dream, Raskolnikov's dream in Dostoevsky's *Crime and Punishment,* where he dreams of a man whipping a horse to death. Here, Raskolnikov (literally, Mr. Schism), is represented by the observor, the horse, and the man beating the horse: this scenario symbolizes his complex relations with his mother and sister.

11. Sigmund Freud, *The Ego and the Id* (New York: Norton, 1962), p. 16.

12. Maurice Merleau-Ponty, *Phenomenology of Perception,* trans. Colin Smith (London: Routledge & Kegan Paul, 1962), p. 237.

13. Sami-Ali, *Corps réel, corps imaginaire* (Paris: Dunod, 1984); see especially chapter 1, "Corps et identite: A propos d'un cas de dépersonalisation," pp. 4–24.

14. Ibid., p. 8.

15. Ibid.

16. Ibid., p. 15.

17. See chapter 6, Formations of Subjectivity and Sexual Identity.

18. See Salvador Dali, "L'Ane pourri" (1930), in *Oui: La révolution paranoiaque-critique* (Paris: Denöel/Gonthier, 1971), pp. 155–60. The relations between Dali's "paranoic-critical method" and Lacan's metapsychology have been widely noted. See Patrice Schmitt, "De la psychose paranoiaque dans ses rapports avec Salvador Dali," in *Salvador Dali* (Paris: Centre Georges Pompidou, 1979), pp. 262–66.

19. Sami-Ali, *Corps réel, corps imaginaire,* p. 18.

20. Ibid., p. 23.

21. Ibid., p. 22.

22. J. Laplanche and J.-B. Pontalis, entry on "Acting Out," in *Vocabulaire de la psychanalyse* (Paris: Presses Universitaires de France, 1973), p. 7.

23. On the relations between conscious and unconscious staging, and the problem of the relation between psychoanalytic and theatrical structures, see Jean-François Lyotard, "The Unconscious as Mise-en-scène," in *Performance in Postmodern Culture,* ed. Michel Benamou and Charles Caramello (Madison: Coda Press, 1977).

24. André Bazin, "Theater and Cinema, Part II," in *What is Cinema?* vol 1, trans. Hugh Gray (Berkeley: Univ. of California Press, 1967), p. 99.

25. Ibid., p. 113.

26. See Émile Benveniste, "De la subjectivité dans le langage," in *Problèmes de linguistique générale,* vol. 1 (Paris: Gallimard, 1966), pp. 257–66.

27. See especially Jacques Lacan's appropriation of Hegel, notably in "The Function and Field of Speech and Language in Psychoanalysis," in *Écrits,* trans. Alan Sheridan (New York: Norton, 1977), pp. 30–113; and "From Interpretation to the Transference," chap. 19 of *The Four Fundamental Concepts of Psycho-analysis,* trans. Alan Sheridan (New York: Norton, 1981), pp. 244–60.

28. Emmanuel Levinas, *Totality and Infinity,* trans. Alphonso Lingis (Pittsburgh: Duquesne Univ. Press, 1969), esp. "Ethics and the Face," pp. 194–219.

29. Stephen Heath, "Film Performance," in *Questions of Cinema* (Bloomington: Indiana Univ. Press. 1981). pp. 115–16.

30. Ibid., p. 124.

31. See Allen S. Weiss "Cartesian Simulacra," *Persistance of Vision* 5 (1987): and Annette Michelson, "Frampton's Sieve," *October* 32 (1985).

32. We should remember, in comparison, that in "A Case of Paranoia Running Counter to the Psychoanalytical Theory of the Disease," the woman believed that certain noises which she heard were caused by a photographer and his assistant who were presumedly hiding behind the curtains in the room where she met her lover, ready to photograph her in a compromising position.

33. The problem of multiple identification in spectatorial construction has not yet been fully worked out in relation to the cinema, but has been approached in several theoretical works, notably in Raymond Bellour, "Psychosis, Neurosis, Perversion"; and Janet Bergstrom, "Enunciation and Sexual Difference," both in *Camera Obscura* 3–4 (1979). The problem of the inmixing of different narratives in a given work may be fruitfully investigated in the light of Bahktin's theory of heteroglossia.

34. Umberto Eco, *"Intentio Lectoris," Differentia* 2 (1988): 151.

35. Roland Barthes, "Les sorties du texte," in *Le bruissement de la langue* (Paris: Seuil, 1984), p. 273.

36. See chapter 6.

Chapter 8. Lucid Intervals

I wish to thank Therese Lichtenstein and Christopher Phillips for their extremely helpful suggestions in editing this article.

1. Michel Tournier, "Veronica's Shrouds," in *The Fetishist,* trans. Barbara Wright (New York: New American Library, 1983). On the relation between the Shroud of Turin and photography, see Patrick Maynard, "The Secular Icon: Photography and the Functions of Images," *The Journal of Aesthetics and Art Criticism* 42, no. 2 (1983): 155–66.

2. Roland Barthes, *La chambre claire* (Paris: Gallimard/Seuil, 1980), p. 141.

3. Philippe Dubois, *L'Acte photographique* (Brussels: Éditions Labor, 1983), pp. 90–91. Dubois refers specifically in this discussion to the disquieting, ambiguous photographic index of death in Michelangelo Antonioni's film *Blow-Up.*

4. Pierre Klossowski, "On the Collaboration of Demons in the Work of Art," trans. Paul Foss and Allen S. Weiss, in *Phantasm and Simulacra,* ed. Paul Foss, Paul Taylor, and Allen S. Weiss, *Art & Text* 18 (July 1985): 9. This special issue on

the works of Klossowski also contains related articles by Paul Foss, Alphonso Lingis, Chantal Thomas, and Allen S. Weiss.

5. Ibid.

6. Pierre Klossowski, "Du tableau en tant que simulacre," in *La Ressemblance* (Marseille: Editions Ryôan-ji, 1984), p. 76.

7. Ibid., p. 77; cf. Nietzsche, "On Truth and Lie in an Extra-Moral Sense."

8. Ibid., p. 78.

9. Pierre Klossowski, "La décadence du nu," in *La Ressemblance,* p. 64. Indeed, Klossowski effected the presentation of his own phantasms in photography and film, both based on his fictional and critical works. See Pierre Zucca's photography for Klossowski's *La monnaie vivante* (Paris: Losfeld, 1970), and the special issue of *Obliques: Roberte au cinéma* (Paris: Editions Borderie, 1978) on Klossowski and Zucca's film, *Roberte Interdite.*

10. Walter Benjamin, "The Work of Art in the Age of Mechanical Reproduction," trans. Harry Zohn, in *Illuminations* (New York: Schocken, 1973), p. 221.

11. Ibid., p. 223. The main proponent of statistical theory as a critical mode is Jean Baudrillard, especially in *In the Shadow of the Silent Majorities,* trans. Paul Foss, Paul Patton, and John Johnston (New York: Semiotext(e), 1983); much earlier, in the 1950s, probability theory was utilized in artistic production, as in Iannis Xenakis's stochastic (probabilistic) music, such as his *Pithoprakta* (1955–56). On the relations between criminological photography and statistics in the nineteenth century, see Allan Sekula, "The Body and the Archive," *October* 39 (1986).

12. Jean Baudrillard, *L'échange symbolique et la mort* (Paris: Gallimard, 1976), p. 115.

13. Jean Baudrillard, *Simulacres et simulation* (Paris: Galilée, 1981), p. 10.

14. Ibid., p. 17.

15. Baudrillard, *In the Shadow,* p. 36.

16. Ibid., p. 10.

17. Baudrillard, *L'échange symbolique,* p. 112.

18. The classic texts on narrative fascination and the ideological structure of the cinematic apparatus are: Laura Mulvey, "Visual Pleasure and Narrative Cinema" *Screen* (1975), and Jean-Louis Baudry, "Effets idéologiques produits par l'appareil de base," *Cinétheque* 7–8.

19. Andre Bazin, *What is Cinema?* vol. 1, trans. Hugh Gray (Berkeley: Univ. of California Press, 1967).

20. Craig Owens, "The Allegorical Impulse: Toward a Theory of Postmodernism (part 2)" *October* 13 (1980): 80.

21. Annette Michelson, "About *Snow,*" *October* 8 (1979): 123. On the importance of a theory of simulacra in the investigation of the transcendental subject, see Marc Richir, *Recherches phénoménologiques (I, II, III): Foundation pour la phénoménologie transcendantale* (Brussels: Éditions Ousia, 1981). Briefly stated: the transcendental ego only appears as an illusion, ungraspable in itself, always masked by the psychological ego. This illusion—an *ontological simulacrum*—is investigated by transcendental phenomenology as a *poetics of origins,* an *art of simulation.* The field of originary ontological phantasma is revealed in the simulations

produced by the transcendental phenomenological reduction, where the generation of variations accords with the figurative structure of the *as if*—the *simile.*

22. Roland Barthes, "Change the Object Itself," trans. Stephen Heath, in *Image, Music, Text* (New York: Hill & Wang, 1977), p. 167.

23. Charles Sanders Peirce, "Logic as Semiotic: The Theory of Signs," in *Philosophical Writings of Peirce,* ed. Justus Buchler (New York: Dover, 1955). On contemporary aesthetic theory of the sign, and especially its indexical aspect in photography, see Rosalind Krauss, "Notes on the Index, parts I and II," in *The Originality of the Avant-Garde and Other Modernist Myths* (Cambridge, Mass.: MIT Press, 1985); and Dubois, *L'Acte photographique:* the first chapter of this work, "De la vérisimilitude à l'index" (co-authored with Geneviève van Cauwenberge), is an excellent history of the problematic, to which this section of my article is indebted.

24. Roland Barthes, "The Photographic Message," in *Image, Music, Text,* p. 17.

25. Dubois, *L'Acte photographique,* p. 49.

26. Barthes, *La chambre claire,* p. 165.

27. Dubois, *L'Acte photographique,* p. 80.

28. Douglas Crimp, "The Photographic Activity of Postmodernism," *October* 15 (1981), p. 98. On the postmodernist photographic practices of Sherrie Levine, Cindy Sherman, Barbara Kruger, and Martha Rosler, see also Craig Owens, "The Allegorical Impulse"; on the significance of the fact that these major postmodernist photographers are all women, see Craig Owens, "The Discourse of Others: Feminists and Postmodernism," in Hal Foster, *The Anti-Aesthetic* (Port Townsend, Wash.: Bay Press, 1983). On the Use of text as icon, see Allen S. Weiss, "Cartesian Simulacra," in *Persistence of Vision* (1987).

29. On the narrative structure of Muybridge's *Studies in Human Locomotion,* see Hollis Frampton, "Eadweard Muybridge: Fragments of a Tesseract," in *Circles of Confusion* (Rochester: Visual Studies Workshop Press, 1983), and Marta Braun, "Muybridge's Scientific Fictions," *Studies in Visual Communication,* 10, no. 3 (1984). We should note here the influence of Marey's chronophotography on both Marcel Duchamp and the Italian Futurists, Duchamp's work especially having had great repercussions on the transition from modernism to postmodernism. On Duchamp's use of photography, see Jean Clair, *Duchamp et la photographie* (Paris: Chêne, 1977).

30. We might remember that the antihumanism of post-structuralist thought— transformed from Heideggerian phenomenology to Derridian deconstruction— founds the "death of the subject" and the "death of the author" on the Nietzschean "death of God." This, in fact, is the central theme of Klossowski's entire oeuvre. We might also remember that post-structuralism and postmodernism are not homologous terms: in fact, the object of most post-structuralist research and criticism, especially at its height in the *Tel Quel* group, is modernist art: postmodernist works are noticably neglected.

The key texts on postmodernism as an epochal shift are those of Jean-François Lyotard, Fredric Jameson, and Jürgen Habermas. See especially the entire issue of *New German Critique* 33, entitled *Modernity and Postmodernity* (1984).

Chapter 9. Broken Voices, Lost Bodies

1. Jacques Lacan, "Le stade du miroir comme formateur de la fonction du Je" (1949), in *Écrits* 1 (Paris: Seuil, 1966), p. 94.

2. Geert Lovink, "The Theory of Mixing: An Inventory of Free Radio Techniques in Amsterdam," in *Mediamatic* 6, no. 4 (1992): 225.

3. Eugène Nicole, *Les larmes de pierre* (Paris: Bourin, 1991), pp. 22–25.

4. Gregory Whitehead, "Radio Art Le Mômo," in *Book for the Unstable Media* ('s-Hertogenbosch: V-2 Organization, 1992), p. 114.

5. See Jacques Attali, *Noise: The Political Economy of Music,* trans. Brian Massumi (Minneapolis: Univ. of Minnesota Press, 1985), p. 91. (French ed: *Bruits: Essai sur l'économie politique de la musique* [Paris: P.U.F., 1977], sec. on "Frozen Speech.")

6. Cited in Attali, *Noise,* p. 91.

7. Ibid., p. 127; emphasis in the original.

8. Gregory Whitehead, "Principia Schizophonica: On Noise, Gas, and the Broadcast Disembody," *Art & Text* 37 (1990): 60.

9. Christof Migone, "Language is the Flower of the Mouth: With Special Guest the Radio Contortionist as Flavour of the Month," *Musicworks* 53 (Toronto, 1992): 45, a special issue on "Radiophonics," ed. Dan Lander.

10. Gregory Whitehead, "Whos's There?: Notes on the Materiality of Radio," *Art & Text* 31 (1989): 12.

11. Michel Chion, *La voix au cinéma* (Paris: Éditions de l'Étoile, 1982), pp. 25–33.

12. Whitehead, "Whos's There?" p. 12.

13. Alberto Savinio, "Psyche," in *The Lives of the Gods,* trans. James Brook (London: Atlas, 1991), p. 8.

14. Gregory Whitehead, "Holes in the Head: A Theatre for Radio Operations," *Performing Arts Journal* 39 (1991): 90–91.

15. Gregory Whitehead, "Radio Art Le Mômo: Gas Leaks, Shock Needles and Death Rattles," *Public* 4–5 (Toronto, 1990–91), a special issue on sound.

16. Paul Virilio, "The Museum of Accidents," *Public* 2 (1989): 81–85; first published in *Art Press* 102 (1986): 13–14.

17. Cited in Rebecca Coyle, "Sound and Speed in Convocation," *Continuum* 6, no. 1 (Murdoch, Australia, 1992): 131, a special issue on "Radio-Sound," ed. Toby Miller.

18. Gregory Whitehead, "Pressures of the Unspeakable: A Nervous System for the City of Sydney," *Continuum* 6, no. 1: 115.

19. Ibid., p. 116.